Learning

Accelerated Learning Guide to Increasing Your
Ability to Learn, Problem-solving Skills and Better
Memory

(Master the Art of Getting Straight a's)

Mark Frank

Published by Rob Miles

© **Mark Frank**

All Rights Reserved

Brain Training: Accelerated Learning Guide to Increasing Your Ability to Learn, Problem-solving Skills and Better Memory (Master the Art of Getting Straight a's)

ISBN 978-1-7771171-7-7

Legal & Disclaimer

The information contained in this book is not designed to replace or take the place of any form of medicine or professional medical advice. The information in this book has been provided for educational and entertainment purposes only.

The information contained in this book has been compiled from sources deemed reliable, and it is accurate to the best of the Author's knowledge; however, the Author cannot guarantee its accuracy and validity and cannot be held liable for any errors or omissions. Changes are periodically made to this book. You must consult your doctor or get professional medical advice before using any of the suggested remedies, techniques, or information in this book.

Table of Contents

Introduction

The world is only becoming bigger, especially when it comes to knowledge. Knowledge is power, which means the more you know, the better opportunities you will present yourself with in life!

The following chapters will discuss many strategies that will help you to learn brand-new concepts at accelerated speeds. From discovering how memory works to effective methods for absorbing lots of new information, your open-book of a brain will be filled with valuable knowledge in no time!

Every effort was made to ensure this book is full of as much useful information as possible, please enjoy!

Chapter 1: The Psychology of Learning - How Does Learning Work?

A) The functioning of the brain - learning channels

The human brain is a miracle and extraordinary. However, its capacity and functionality are limited. Neurosciences, however, provide insights into the functions of the brain, which also play a part in learning and which are developed using learning methods that can enormously increase the effectiveness of learning.

Through the sense organs, we collect informations that are processed and stored in the brain. Depending on the quality of the information we either store it in the short, ultrasound or long-term memory. How long we store information depends not only on its importance for us, but first of all on how the information came first into the brain. The probability of keeping information is roughly different:

Information	Probability of retention
Learn it yourself	90%
Tell through / explain	70%
Listen + see	50%
see	30%
hear	20%

This leads to two important consequences for learning.

1.**Active information acquisition** (eg recount) is more effective than passive (eg see).

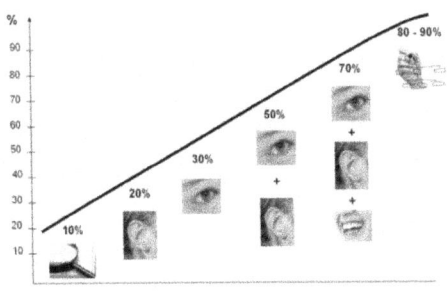

2.The more **channels** that are addressed at the same **time** , the more the information is retained. Anyone who wants to explain something to someone else, must have understood this before, eg read or heard. If you try and use something, the actual information is already linked to the whole process, which is why the result is more firmly anchored in the brain, as if it had only been observed by someone else.

The learning channels

Learning channels are the various **ways to record information** . There are four learning channels:

· Read

· To hear [to be read aloud, to hear from the tape]

· See [eg graphics, pictures, watching movies, creating inner images]

· Talking [pretending to fabricate oneself, explaining to someone or themselves, summarizing matter verbally]

· Acting [even starting with the material, eg constructing own examples, making graphics, tinkering, etc.]

The graphic shows you how effective the individual learning channels and their combinations are. The left scale shows the proportion of the retained facts when they are recorded over the learning channel.

As you can see, the combination of the different learning channels can increase your learning success. This is because the retention is added and you learn faster and more efficiently. If you want to learn something, you should use as many learning channels as possible. However, **not every learning channel is suitable for every information** . For example, it is relatively difficult to follow mathematical calculations only through hearing.

Finally, it is to be noted that **the channel of one's own action** is indeed the most elaborate, but also **the most effective learning channel** . So if you really want to keep something, you can achieve it best through practical exercises and application.

B) Learning type

When learning, our senses (seeing, hearing, smelling, tasting, feeling) play an important role because everything we learn is absorbed by our sense organs. In doing so, we use the sense organs, which are the most pronounced. And so it happens that some of us learn best by reading something, looking at images or graphics, others by listening, and others themselves have to write down something or talk with others to keep something.

Modern learning research distinguishes between the following **4 types of learning** : **auditory** , **visual** , **communicativ e** and **motor-driven** , depending on the sense organ of the learning material.

Learning by listening - the auditory learning type

The auditive learning type listens and eases information with the ears. He can easily follow oral explanations and process them. This makes it particularly easy for him to understand what teachers, lecturers, seminar leaders, etc. say and explain. The auditory type almost always needs an oral explanation for a panel or diagram. Only then does what he sees become coherent and comprehensible for him. Auditive learning types can learn very well with the help of audio books, listening CD's. On the other hand, reading often means a real concentration.

By the way : Music can lend wings to the auditory learning type.

Learning to see - the visual learning type

Visual learning types rely primarily on the eyes during learning. They learn best by using (looking) pictures, illustrations or graphics and by reading information. For them, it is usually a child's play, to understand board pictures or even complicated diagrams. They love to write and remember what they have read and seen.

The visual learning type needs a nice and orderly learning environment. He is very easily distracted by disorder.

Learning aids : books, sketches, colored pictures, mind maps, learning posters, videos, learning maps

Learning by movement - the motor learning type

The motor learning type learns best by doing "doing" - that is, learning by doing ! He "works out" the learning material in the truest sense of the word. He remembers excellently the information he has received through movement, action and feeling.

He learns particularly well when he can move around learning! For example, he runs up and down the room while he is learning. He also works a lot with gestures and facial expressions. He loves experiment and has to touch everything. For motorized learning types it is a force effort to have to sit at the desk for more than half an hour at a time.

Learning aids : (rhythmic) movements, imitating, group activities, roll games

Learning through conversations - the communicative learning type

The communicative learning type learns best by asking questions, giving answers, or discussing points of view. The exchange and the conversation with others is his learning elixir. In this way he understands connections and meanings best. He likes to take an active part in the classroom and learns in a group of like-minded people with whom they can exchange ideas about the material to be learned.

Communicative learning types are very difficult to learn by themselves.

Learning aids : **dialogues** , discussions, learning groups, question-answer games

How is each learning type most effective? - Learning tips for each type

Now that we know what types of learning there are, here for each learning type a few practical learning tips:

If you are part of the auditory learning type, the following tips will help you learn:

· Read texts aloud! What you read quietly, will not hang so well with you. This is especially useful when learning vocabulary!

· Many auditive learning types help to conduct self-talk during learning. This goes from explaining a task to the sound of an imagined song as a learning material.

· Take your own learning cards or mp3s! On the one hand, you speak the learning material aloud, on the other hand you explain the learning material, which also helps you to learn. Then you can listen to the learning material so often, until you have internalized it.

· Always look for a pleasant noise when learning. Depending on the disposition, music can support learning - as long as it is not a disturbing noise!

If you are a visual learning type, you can do the following:

· Write as much as possible in the classroom! What has not been left behind by the explanations of your teachers can be read at home in peace.

· Paint your sketches, mind maps, diagrams! Put the material in pictures. You understand the connections much better and you can easily remember, because you have the learning material stored in pictures.

· See pictures or other illustrations on the subject in textbooks or on the Internet! The Internet has pictures of almost every learning material!

· Card types are particularly suitable for learning especially when learning vocabulary. Many cards with only one vocabulary can be learned particularly well. If you also paint small pictures on the card types, you can remember the words even better.

· Write the stuff in your own words! Not just reading, writing also helps visual learning types while learning.

· Create your own learning posters, where you summarize the learning material. Hang them where you are particularly common - for example, next to the bed or in the bathroom. So you learn so to speak, by the way!

If you are interested in the motorized learning type, the following tips can help:

· Try to find learning materials to touch! These can be experiment boxes or models, but also scrabble stones to learn grammar, vocabulary or spelling

· Invite your friends to learn and build or build intuitive learning material. Rolling games also help you learn specific situations.

· Play with the learning material! Try to incorporate so many things from your lessons into your free time!

· Move while learning! Runs up and down in the room, repeating the learner's material and completing it with gestures and facial expressions. Give your hands something to do, playing for example with a ball or turning a pen between your fingers.

If you belong to the communicative learning type, the following tips help:

· Learn, if possible, not alone! Invite friends or learn with your parents and siblings. Explain the problem and try to find solutions together with them.

· Play rolls games (for example, an interview) where you talk about a specific course. Try to discuss the subject as comprehensively as possible.

· Talk with friends about the learning material - best before homework. Discuss and develop the topic together. Speak about all the points that come to your mind.

· Play a quiz! Think about questions on a specific topic, write them on cards and then play with your friends, for example, "Who is a millionaire?" So learning is really fun.

Everyone should know their learning type

If you are familiar with your learning type and take the appropriate learning-type tips, you will learn faster, easier and more successfully. In addition, the probability that you will remember the lessons learned will also increase when you need it.

But how do I find out which type of learning I am?

Very simple: Makes a learning type test.

By the way, no one learns with "only one meaning". We are sensual beings and always experience the world with all our senses.

The more senses we activate in learning, the better we can internalize and recall the learning material. So try to include as many senses as possible in the learning process, regardless of what type of learning you are. The more senses involved in learning, the better we anchor the learning material and the better we remember.

C) Learning curve / forgetting curve - Why do we forget?

The learning curve indicates the learning success in relation to the time spent. An ability increases when one applies them again and again or knowledge strengthens itself, if one continuously increases this. What appears to be hard for the first time, has proven to be the most experienced on the hundredth time. The entry into a new topic is often quite tedious, if there is a certain basic knowledge and a basic understanding of the topic, it can be more easily filled by more concrete expertise. Learning success does not take place until the time.

The forgetting curve, on the other hand, indicates the degree of forgetting as a function of time. If we do not touch a once-created ability, it reverts. What applies to muscle building also applies to learning. **Knowledge must be applied**, in the ideal case even multiplied, otherwise it decreases. Our brain is regularly flooded in everyday life with stimuli and information, the most of which are of no great importance. This is why most of this information can only be found in the ultra-short-term memory and can not be retrieved in a short time. It is said that after about an hour already about half of the learned has forgotten again, after one day already two-thirds and after a week about 75-80%.

It is therefore not enough to have learned a chapter and to have appropriated the content. If the examination, in which exactly the knowledge is questioned, only takes place in a few months, the danger is great that it has become gaps. **Therefore, it is important to consolidate what is learned through repetition and application in the brain** and to learn continuously.

This also explains why our memory fails us sometimes:

You meet an old acquaintance and talk splendidly. But unfortunately you do not remember what the person is called. Or you cannot remember whether you have already salted what you are cooking or where you placed your wallet. Your memory will leave you in the lurch. But what is the reason for this? Why does our memory forget information? The answer: To function, our memory must also forget things.

Our memory MUST be forgotten
The short-term memory can not store an unlimited amount of information. That is why information fades. If we were to keep everything, our brain would be completely overloaded. Everything that is unimportant, we can immediately forget. This theory, however, does not apply to long-term memory.

Our memory overlays information
In long-term memory, one information may cover another. Especially when two information is similar.

We do not rummage
Possibly information is stored somewhere in the memory, but can simply no longer find or retrieve. For this theory, thinks that

thought-provoking can help to recall events or information.

Emotions bind memories
We remember things very well when they are connected with strong feelings. In the case of equivalent positive or negative emotions, we have memories in our memory, with which we associate positive. That is why many people tend to glorify the past as a "good, old time." Even if we repeatedly remember things, we forget them more slowly.

In addition, events are better remembered when they are associated with many sensory impressions. In addition, we remember more easily when we are in the same mood or situation in which we have received information. If we are sad, the unsightly events are more present than the joyous experiences.

... Stress kills them
If you have a lot of stress, forget things faster. Also physical or mental stress, such as nervousness, are stressful for us. Everyone knows this from his school

days: we sit in a test and can not remember anything we've learned. Guilt of this is probably a stress hormone, which hinders the work of nerve cells.

But other influences, such as drugs and alcohol, also affect memory. In the end there is another factor that weakens our memory: age. But you can counter this: the more effort we have to train the brain, the easier it is for us to retrieve information.

The forgetting curve: after a week, three quarters of what you learned are forgotten

The whole thing has something to do with the so-called forgetting curve. This is exactly what the German psychologist Hermann Ebbinghaus found in his **self-experiments** :

· After about **20 minutes** , he had already forgotten 40%.

· After **an hour** , the half-life of knowledge decreased to 45 percent.

- After **one day,** he recalled a third (34 percent).

- After only **six days** , the memory capacity has shrunk to a decent 23 percent - in the long run, we only keep **15 percent** of what we have learned. What a pity.

How to stop forgetting?

Every day our **brain is** flooded by a huge amount of information. If we try to remember all the information, our brain would burn like a fuse. For us, forgetting is at the same time an essential part of our lives and learning.

So that our brain does not run hot, 100 billion nerve **cells process** thousands of impulses every second fraction of the pulse and filter new information: important things are permanently stored and unimportant are immediately discarded.

When we speak of **memory** , we mean the ability to organize, store, and retrieve information. It is a complex network of different areas of our brain. When we notice something, a connection between different nerves is established. This connection is crucial for us to learn something new.

(D) The quality of the material to be learned.

It is easier for most people to notice material which is rationally easily explained, intuitive, and visually conceivable. While abstract things are often more difficult to understand and remember. Things (body of knowledge) with a large practical relevance remains adherent rather than pure theory.

Analyze the material to be learned and provide an overview of **the type of knowledge or learning material** they are dealing with. This makes it easier to plan how to deal with the material.

TIP : If possible, use several channels to record knowledge. The more actively they deal with the substance, the better it remains in the memory.

21

Analyze their own learning type and adapt their learning strategy to it - not vice versa. Keep in mind that "all beginnings are difficult". When the foundations sit, the detailed knowledge is relatively easy.

Chapter 2: Accelerated Learning can Change your Life

What is Accelerated Learning?

Accelerated learning is a type of learning that helps an individual excel in whatever they are trying to learn. Obviously, accelerated learning offers a much more vigorous program compared to mainstream learning, but the benefits that you gain from it greatly outweigh the downsides. The key aspect of accelerated learning is that it is accelerated. It's all about learning quickly rather than slowly and thoroughly. Of course, an individual doesn't get the same thorough learning experience, but they are still offered exactly the same learning content, but just in a different way.

Accelerated Learning Vs Mainstream Learning

Mainstream Learning

Mainstream classes are offered to the majority of the educated populace. The upside to these type of classes is that students and individuals are offered a thorough learning course. The key difference between accelerate classes and mainstream classes is the time-frame individuals are given to learn a subject. The downsides to mainstream classes is that the quality of learning is much lower than accelerate classes. This is because there is generally more students in the mainstream classes, and these students as well as the students aren't as locked in as students and teachers that are in accelerated classes.

Accelerate Learning

Accelerate learning is generally offered to students and individuals that excel in mainstream classes. It gives these individuals the opportunity to apply themselves without having to worry about the distractions that are offered from mainstream classes. Of course, accelerate learning is much more stressful than mainstream learning, but this is only because people that are in accelerate classes take their education much more serious than the majority of people in mainstream classes. Accelerate learning offers an individual everything that they'd learn from a mainstream class, but at a much quicker rate and they are also offered other aspects of a subject also. It is for people who are willing to go the extra mile.

Accelerate Learning is the Best way to Learning

It is no secret that accelerate learning is the best way to learn. The best part about accelerate learning and accelerate classes is that people are passionate about your learning and learning in general. The environment is a perfect one to be in if you are searching for a place to learn without the distractions that mainstream learning offers an individual. Of course, it is stressful to be in an accelerate class, but it is much better to be stressing over the work instead of stressing over actually getting work or people not caring at all about your education. Accelerate learning is the future.

Chapter 3: LEARNING

Learning is a commonly used term. Often you stumble upon him, but mostly we associate school or education with that word. But what is 'learning'? The acquisition of theoretical knowledge certainly counts, including the acquisition of motor skills.

The everyday use of the word 'learning' aims primarily towards 'learning content'. Content includes knowledge, skills, but also attitudes.

In addition to content, other processes may also play a role in learning. In the definition presented later,

"learning means a change in experience and behaviour due to individual experiences in or with the environment."

There is the talk of change, with a change not just in learning content. A change in behaviour can also come about through learning processes in which unlearning or even problem-solving processes take centre stage.

On closer inspection, it quickly becomes clear how often we, in reality, learn or how often we on Learned draw:

- Do you have a special (not innate) ability? (For example, dealing with knives and forks - driving a car, writing, speaking?)

- Are you following a hobby?

- Do you have fears?

- Can you find your way around the society or integrate yourself?

- Do you change your behaviour based on experience? (e.g. getting up on Mondays, as there is more traffic?)

Learning is personal. Everyone has their way of learning. The consideration of different learning types and different learning tempi is important.

Learning is a solution and resource-oriented. The view of learning in the cognitive, as well as the social field, should be directed to solutions to resources. What succeeds is emphasized. Success is evidence of meaningful learning strategies and further learning success. This is very motivating.

Learning is doing actively. Doing it yourself, explaining it yourself, developing your ideas, finding solutions yourself, taking notes yourself and explanations are activities that promote sustainable learning.

Learning has to be meaningful. Learning to stock is of limited use. Learning opportunities should already make sense for children and benefit them at the moment.

Learning is slow. Many learning processes need a lot of time. Children must be left this time.

Learning is leaps and bounds. Often, learning processes are not linear. Many learning processes need digestion. This is often not visible, but then suddenly comes to light.

Learning happens with other people. The exchange with others, communication and conflict management in a constructive way are essential elements of learning.

Learning should be sustainable. If learning meets many of these guidelines, it will have a lasting impact.

Learning is recognizing and using learning strategies. Regular thinking about learning strategies promotes the ability to learn successfully again and again.

Learning also happens from mistakes. Mistakes are useful hints for further learning fields. That's why bugs are useful. Errors can be handled constructively.

WHAT IS ACCELERATED LEARNING?

Maybe you are familiar with it, but perhaps not. The term accelerated learning is a term that has been used more often and more frequently in recent years.

Accelerated learning, also known as super learning or accelerated learning, is a collection of methods that ensure that you can absorb information much more quickly.

Accelerated learning, developed by the Bulgarian scientist Lozanov, not only offers you techniques and tips to learn more "brain-friendly", but it also ensures that you will enjoy learning again.

To make learning easier and faster, it is, therefore, essential to enjoy learning.

Chapter 4: Accelerated Learning: The Guidepost Principles

As with any learning method, certain guideposts provide the boundaries of how best to execute the method. While there might be several different ways to achieve the end results, accelerated learning relies on these guideposts to give instructors some guages when dealing with their students.

One of the first guideposts is that learning must involve the whole mind, as well as the body, to achieve the most long-lasting results. When we think of learning as merely involving the head, we shortchange ourselves both as teachers and students. In reality, we need to immerse ourselves with all of our senses, emotions and of course, the various information and data receptors available to our students. Learning a new skill might even involve taking time away from other activities to give the immersion process our undivided attention. Yet, for many who follow this guidepost in their learning journey, they find it leads to much success and long term retention.

Another critical guidepost is the recognition of the building of a knowledge base as a creation on the part of the learner themselves. A student cannot consume knowledge but must build it as part of a larger learning process. When one is learning something, the student is putting in place new neural pathways, as well as integrating the information into the knowledge they already have. The result is the addition of new meanings, new patterns in terms of electro/chemical interactions and of course, new structures in how we think about the world based on newly acquired information. Thus, a student needs to feel empowered to build this knowledge base by means of their instructor, not stifled and thus unmotivated to create knowledge for themselves. This guidepost should cause the teacher to reflect on the importance of creating a positive and inviting learning environment right from the start.

Collaboration is another important guidepost of accelerated learning. Good learning methods are typically based on a social, collaborative platform. Our various interactions often contribute to the creation of our knowledge base. Students acquire so much information from their peers that it is critical to foster a sense of collaboration, instead of pitting students against each other in a competitive learning style. Isolated individuals will take longer to absorb information or new skills. For example, many colleges encourage students to build study groups. This method recognizes how important collaboration and cooperation are to the success of any student.

Learning often happens on multiple levels. This particular guidepost focuses on how information is acquired, not in a linear fashion, but essentially all at once. The brain is often processing multiple bits of information from the senses at the exact same time. Learning can and should occur in exactly the same fashion. Therefore, any teacher using the accelerated learning method should be focused on getting their students to learn through their conscious, sub-conscious, mental and physical states. Thus, the students is using all their body's receptors to gather the necessary information that will result in their building a large knowledge base. The brain can often be referred to as a parallel processor, so it thrives when challenged to compile and analyze information at a rapid rate from multiple platforms. A student who is learning on multiple levels can find it energizing, plus it contributes to long term retention on the brain's part.

For those who are learning a new skill, nothing is better than actually doing the work themselves. The brain can then be engaged on a multiple level platform. The five senses are completely in use as part of the learning process. When a student is provided feedback after completing a job or procedure, they are able to integrate and reflect on the feedback. Thus, adjustments can be made to the procedure or the work method to build on the student's knowledge base. Imagine working at a factory or another job that requires you to learn multiple processes at the same time. When trying to learn the task, repeating it frequently perhaps with instructions can really drive it into one's brain. Long term retention will be just one of the results, along with the satisfaction of having acquired a new skill.

Reimmersing oneself in a task after receiving feedback, which benefits from reflection. Students often find themselves better able to relate to information when presented in a concrete fashion, versus the use of abstract or hypothetical situations that might have little bearing on the current student's needs. As a student, one needs to look for real life applications of their new knowledge to keep it fresh but also to maintain their retention level.

Understand that another important guidepost is based on the emotional state of the student themselves. Stop for a minute and imagine a time when you have been particularly frustrated or angry. Did you try to pick up a new skill or add to your knowledge base during that time period? It probably did not end well. Can you even remember the skill you were attempting to learn? Most of us would reply with a negative to that question. On the other hand, when we have attempted to learn something while in a positive mood. The result is more affective knowledge building, plus there is better long term retention. Therefore, a student needs to approach their learning process with a positive attitude. Negative attitudes make it hard to grow and create a knowledge base. Learning in a dreary, stressful or painful fashion is not likely to last, but is more likely to be inhibited. When learning is based on a joyful, engaging and relaxing environment, the student is able to learn with both quality, as well as significant quantity.

Finally, one needs to remember that the brain does not function as a word processor. Instead, it is able to function as an image processor. Thus, the brain can consume large quantities of information via its entire nervous system. So do not sell your students short, just because there is a large amount of information to be absorbed. They can do it. To assist them, use concrete images versus verbal abstractions. If the information a teacher must impart is primarily verbal, then the teacher would need to translate the information into a variety of concrete images to assist their students in absorbing the necessary information.

As we have seen throughout our coverage of these guideposts, the most critical thing a teacher can do is listen to their students. What is working and what is not? Find out from the students and be willing to tweak your methods whenever necessary. Using these guideposts will help a teacher to create an environment that allows their students to freely build a knowledge base of both skills and data.

Still one needs to help their students keep mentally sharp. There are many methods for assisting someone to build their mental skills, sharpening both IQ and overall mental clarity. We will explore some of these methods and how as a bonus, they can provide memory enhancement as well.

Chapter 5: Learnacy

When most people reflect on their learning experiences, they imagine the hardest parts of those experiences. But you are wiser! You now understand why your mind needs to be activated before you begin to learn. You now know that you require a wider knowledge of the art of learning, or how you learn to learn.

Let us assume that you are prepared and powered up to learn. What are the ways you can enhance the way you utilize your mind? How can you make sure that you become an efficient learner? Now that you have a sound knowledge about the brain and why it is a waste of energy if you are not mentally prepared and enthusiastic about starting, this section contains some of the solutions and the major techniques.

Perhaps, we can adopt a reductionist view of learning that presumes that it is basically the total of a few techniques and training. Yet this is obviously not true.

Learning is intricate and difficult to master. The techniques are only a minor part of the whole. Assuming learning was an iceberg, the method used would be viewed overhead. What is underneath the water—the emotional and mental self-knowledge that we have been making an effort to discover and the areas yet to be discovered—would be the major component of the ice hidden from external view.

The moment when you realize that you are intentionally prepared to start learning when you recognize that you can't do the things you desire to, you would be required to pass through some phases to be adequately qualified in your field of study.

Take driving a car for instance. To start with, you do not even realize that you want to learn to drive. Then you become aware that you can't do something you would like to do. Maybe as a teenager, you have observed one of your parents driving and started imagining what it would feel like. Or you had an elder sibling who you believe to be having more fun as compared to you because they could drive. Thus, you learn how to do it, but attempt every part of the process with utmost care, carefully looking in the mirror, using the indicator and finally setting out in the road in an almost robotic manner, driving forward and backward as you try to reverse the car into a compact parking area.

Eventually, you would be able to do it all without even being conscious of what you are doing. You can change gears while driving, spontaneously look in your mirror at intervals and making conversations while doing this.

To put this differently, you have done a turnaround from not recognizing that you were incompetent as a driver to being very proficient that you just drive without even focusing your attention on it. Most analysts agree that this is the order of progression:

Unconscientious incompetence becomes conscientious incompetence, which then evolves into conscientious competence, and lastly, unconscientious competence.

This progression is the key to learning and learning to learn. In spite of the increasing interest in this process, methodical exploration and definition of this area have not been achieved. The following are the major elements of the idea of learnancy—they are relevant and crucial to learning.

Establishing the amount of learning done in solitude versus that done as part of a group

Deciding to learn on the web

Reading books about learning and utilizing the media

Making plans to use a particular method and ensuring it is used

Imbibing how others behave or act

Differentiating between formal and informal learning experiences

Writing a journal of your learning

Repeating or reinforcing techniques not frequently used

Establishing how much of learning is active or passive

Studying other people's methods of learning

Dividing learning into sections of "hows"

Constantly expanding your knowledge of learning techniques from all available sources

Recognizing how much of your learning is by retaining facts or information versus observing or trial and error

Resiliently trying to understand now learning methods or techniques until they become less difficult

Routinely exploring your learning styles

Reflecting on both pleasurable and unpleasurable feelings set off by various learning experiences

Concentrating on improving the learning styles of your choice

Experimentally exploring various techniques of learning

Intentionally selecting learning options that require the full use of your abilities

Utilizing mind charts or web diagrams

Deliberately using a learning principle, for instance, the cycle of learning or the concept of multiple intelligence

Thinking deeply on your incentives for learning, the fundamental ones and the ones that drive you

Making use of patterns to switch on your memory

Utilizing various study styles and methods

Realizing the diverse roles individuals play when studying together as a group

Dealing with the feelings and emotions that perfuse learning

Providing an answer to the question, how can I enhance my learning style?

Adapting learning techniques from other people

Coming to terms with unexpected, unintentional occurrences and figuring out how they can impart your learning

Partaking in activities to augment learning skills and/or getting the best out of your weaknesses

Understanding Who You Are as a Learner

It is not surprising that you would want to have a better understanding of your identity. Instances of relevant areas to explore from our research include the following:

Recognizing how much of your learning is done in solitude and as part of a group

Recognizing the amount of passive versus active learning you engage in

Recognizing how much of your learning is assimilating new information versus learning from experience

Learning to Use New Techniques: 5RS

Thus far in this book, you have been taught quite a number of new learning methods, with the inclusion of these "preparing to learn" skills:

Imbibing how others behave or act

Reflecting on both pleasurable and unpleasurable feelings set off by various learning experiences

Thinking deeply on your incentives for learning, the fundamental ones and the ones that drive you

Realizing the diverse roles individuals play when studying together

Dealing with the feelings and emotions that perfuse learning

Almost all the other techniques included in the list are needed to make you more effective as a learner. Let me take a trip down memory lane to the days you were still in school. For the majority of us, the necessary skills or fundamental tools of childhood were referred to as the 3Rs: writing, arithmetic, and reading. Whereas these remain important skills, there are other skills to acquire in this age of knowledge.

Guy Claxton, a British academic has published an engaging deduction of this discussion in **Wise-Up: The Challenge of Lifelong Learning**[1]. He proposes a different set of 3Rs: reflectiveness, resilience, and resourcefulness.

He affirms that the eternal learner should focus on these new key areas of efficiency. They have a wider scope than the previous 3Rs. And that is the truth—they refer to the real life where learning is till infinity and behaviors and skills are more significant than the acquisition of specific knowledge.

I agree with his opinion, though there are two additional relevant areas: recalling and responsiveness. The secret to a lot of our learning is memorization, particularly memorization for methods and approaches instead of memorizing facts. In a global age, memory for facts is progressively less relevant. And it is the ability to adapt that is the genuine quality that continuing learners require in order to transform the manner with which they do things in their lives.

So forget about the old 3Rs, instead, think of the improved 5Rs: recalling, resourcefulness, responsiveness, reflectiveness, and resilience. These skills form the basis for what makes for continued, effective learning in a learner.

Learning All About Learning

Coming to terms with the notion that learnacy is equally as important as numeracy, and literacy creates a natural inclination to want to discover more about theories of learning.

Without any distinction, the most evident way of getting knowledge about learning is by reading books or using another medium to explore the subject further.

For a lot of people, the stage of being conscientiously competent is the most relevant one. If you are curious about maximizing the full potential of your mind, you have to deeply explore books on that subject. Already, you are familiar with the theories that would be vital to this.

There are two evident instances above:

•Differentiating between formal and informal learning

•Comprehending the various roles played by individuals learning together as a group

Paradoxically, learning the art of learning makes it very hard to keep being interested, without putting it into practice. In this same regard, it would be hard to learn about architecture. You might read about how houses were structured in the Middle Ages, although it isn't important to set out and start building one. Without necessarily having to put the theory into practice, your curiosity still remains. This is not the case with learning.

You have to have a firsthand experience of something in order to fully imbibe it. Reading a book about learning to learn instead of actually doing it is eventually going to make you frustrated. You would probably want to apply the knowledge you have gained in your personal activities.

Types of Learning

The concept of learning is so broad that it is easy to generalize it, this, failing to take note that there are different approaches to learning. Imagine a normal working day in your life. Try to figure out the number of various learning you experience. For every category, try to think up a minimum of one example. Now reflect on all your learning last month.

• Formal—attending the university, enrolling for a training program

• Informal—observing a colleague you respect handle a discussion in your family centered on your thoughts about a new movie

• Temporary—trying out a new computer program, constructing a new set of shelves packed flat.

- Permanent—coping with a hard emotional situation, apologizing for wrongdoings

- Externally approved—being awarded a certificate for saving lives, taking an MBA

- For individual interest—learning to tile your bathroom, creating a pond in your garden.

- Compulsory—taking a training course you did not choose, getting an education

- Voluntary—choosing to browse the web, learning to speak French

- Social—learning to play a game as a team, starting a new project with some coworkers.

- Individual—going through a book, browsing the web.

A lot of people have discovered that out of these ten various categories, the components of "informal" learning has the highest number of elements.

Chapter 6: Right on Time

As was said before, everyone have different goals for their lives. Some people want to succeed in the business world, while others desire to be a stay-at-home parent. Some want to fill up their schedule with tons of hobbies, while others just want to make their experience a little bit better through exercise or meditation. Obviously, depending on your goals, you will need to focus on different things in different ways to reach them, but there is one thing that everyone – regardless of their goals – will need to adhere to if they wish to find any sort of success.

This thing (which you may have already guessed based on this particular chapter's title) is that which keeps all of the reality moving forward. It prevents us from remaining in one moment too long; it has been around since before any of us were born and will go on long after we're all gone. If you still haven't figured it out yet, that thing is time.

Yes, when it comes to self-discipline, the familiar minute and hour hands of your average clock can either be your greatest ally or your most dreaded foe depending on how you use it. If we had infinite time to juggle all the things we wanted to do – work, school, relationships, housework, exercise, reading, etc. – there would be no need for self-discipline because we could simply get to these things whenever we were in the mood. But we don't have infinite time in our lives and, thanks to the ancient Egyptians, we only have a measly 24 hours in a single day. Actually, it is an unfortunate truth that in this modern age, we only possess a small fraction of that.

According to most health professionals, the average person needs about eight hours of sleep per night, so after catching those z's, 1/3 of the day is already gone. Given also that the usual 9 am to 5 pm work schedule is what most people have, that leaves the majority of us with just eight hours of free time to make some headway in what we want to do with our lives.

But, we're not finished yet. Let's break it down even more. The average person spends about forty minutes to an hour every day commuting to and from work. On top of that, they'll also spend another hour to two hours every day taking care of their nutrition, hygiene, and – if they're in school – educational needs (i.e. cooking, eating, using the bathroom, doing homework, showering, brushing teeth). After all this is said and done, it is not out of the realm of reason to think that a normal person – after all of their obligations at work or school are done and after their personal needs are taken care of – will be left with something like one to three daily hours to accomplish their goals.

But let's be honest; there are plenty of other ways a person can deplete that time even further in this day and age where we are surrounded by things that are tailor-made to take away our precious minutes.

According to one study, the average American spends about one hour and forty minutes browsing his or her various social media accounts **every day**! I personally had some serious problems with this, and although over ninety minutes a day might seem like an exaggeration, I think it's very much within the realm of possibility to burn away that much of your free time when you check Facebook, Instagram, Twitter, and Snapchat multiple times each throughout the day.

The point is, you have your goals, whatever they may be, but to accomplish them, you actually need to work on them. And to do that, you need to take time. But based on what you've read about how the majority of your day is pretty much totally gone by the time you actually have a free second to pursue your goals, the question may have presented itself: how do I do that? How am I supposed to accomplish my goals which will take a lot of time — time that I myself don't have?

Well here's the good news: although we aren't able to control how much time we are given, we can control what we do with the free time we do have.

In the following four steps, I'm going to outline the ways in which you can put a saddle on your free time so that you can ride that baby all the way to your goals!

1.   Scheduling (actually writing down a list)

Perhaps the most important thing to do in taking control of your free time is to take stock of exactly how much you have and divide it up accordingly by writing it out. This might seem quite obvious, but I can't tell you how many people I know that just have their schedule inside their head and still expect to get everything done. People are prone to forget things, and I hate to break it to those of you who think you can reach maximum productivity this way, but I promise you, sooner or later you too will forget something you otherwise would've remembered had you written it down.

And no, you don't need to keep a notepad and pencil on you at all times, because you know that smartphone of yours? Yeah, the one that's either within arm's reach from you right now, or possibly the thing you're using to read this book with? Well, that thing isn't only a powerful tool to stay connected to the things and people you need connection with; it's also your very own personal assistant that can aid you in making great use of the free time you have so you can start making strides in what you want to accomplish.

All you need to do is open a blank document or list app (I like Evernote) every Sunday night – or before whichever day you want your week to start – and title it: To-Do This Week. Then, simply, write down what it is you want to accomplish that week.

Exercise

Start planning that trip

Declutter the apartment and put some things on Craigslist

Etc.

2. Break it down

Now that you have your list, you need to figure out how much free time you have approximately and how to divide it to accommodate your to-do list accordingly. I find that it helps to split things up into the days of the week, but you can do it however you like.

Example:

Exercise: 3 hours (Monday 7 am-8 am, Wednesday 7 am-8 am, Friday 7 am-8 am)

Start planning that trip: 2 hours (Monday 7 pm-8 pm, Thursday (7 pm-8 pm)

Declutter and sell things online: 2 hours (Tuesday 7 pm-8 pm, Thursday 8 pm-9 pm)

By doing this, you can clearly see when you need to start doing something and for how long you need to do it. This is extremely helpful in accomplishing both short and long-term goals because it allows you to break up the tasks into manageable chunks that don't overwhelm you all at once.

3. Use the rollover method

Starting a new lifestyle can be hard, especially one like increased self-discipline where it's likely to be very different from your old way of doing things. That's why, when starting your list of how you wish to divide up your time, you don't try to do too much too fast. Give yourself a few simple tasks to start with so that you can get into the new groove of doing things. After you've gone a few weeks and you've become comfortable with the number of them, feel free to throw some other things into the mix.

But, as an addendum, if you happen to fail to accomplish everything in a certain week, say, for instance, you did all your written tasks but didn't get around to building that bookshelf, make sure you bring that task over onto the next week you make your to-do list. This ensures that everything you write down gets done eventually. Also, it would be wise to keep a firm number of things on your week-to-week list and not to add another thing to the list until you finish that task from the week before. This helps you to not get bogged down by too many things you weren't able to get to in prior weeks.

4. You just need to do it (even a little)

You may have heard that the hardest step to take on any journey is the first, which is debatable, but one could argue that by simply making the list, you've taken that first step. I, however, would disagree. Until you actually start doing those things that are on your list, you haven't actually begun. Anyone can write some things down, but to actually act on those things shows your dedication to them and starts you on your way to becoming a master of self-discipline.

Despite your best efforts though, there will be problems. Guaranteed. You might have had a bad day at the office, or maybe you didn't get a good night's rest and so aren't feeling mentally "there" enough to work on knocking out the items on your list. You might feel like you won't be able to get anything done, and so you decide to put the list on the backburner and stare at the TV for three hours when you get home.

Although the temptation to do this will be strong, especially when you've had a rough day, I urge you to try and stick to the schedule at least partially. It's a slippery slope when you skip one day because one day turns into two, two turns into three, and before you know it, a month has gone by and your first week of to-dos has gone untouched. This is why it's okay to change the list as you go. If you need to take a half hour off a task you initially planned on spending an hour on, that's okay. Any progress, no matter how minimal, is better than none.

When you find myself lacking the energy to do something on the list, thinking actively about how these things are something you want to do helps. Yes, they may seem like an obligation at first when you're feeling burned out from a hard day, but remember: you were the one who wrote them down in the first place. It may have been you from a few weeks or a month earlier, but it was still you; so, deep down it is definitely you who wants to do these things. Given this, by not doing them, you're not letting anyone down but your own self.

I said it before and I'll say it again here (and probably later on as well): **self-discipline is about building and maintaining good habits.** No matter what your goals are, to accomplish them, you need to do the work that is required of you, and to do that work, you need to get into the habit of doing just it. Habits, my friend, are built by repetition, and repetition is built by – you guessed it – a schedule.

Obviously, we are just mere mortals and don't have the godly power of controlling time; but again, it's not about controlling time itself, but rather what we do with that time. I can promise you that some of the most successful people found their success not by whittling away their extra hours absentmindedly, but by focusing their time like a laser beam towards whatever goal they wished to achieve. And the way in which they did this was almost certainly a concrete schedule that they stuck to like glue. As an added incentive, I've found that in sticking to a solid schedule, my days stopped flying by so fast because I was more aware of time rather than just barely noticing it as it went by me. This makes sense too, because in the words of the great Leonardo da Vinci, **"Time stays long enough for those who use it."**

Chapter 7: Steps to Increase Reading Speed

There is no doubt that you could accomplish so much more in your daily life and beyond by reading at a faster rate. Taking in all of the information that we see every day can be time consuming, and you can use that time for much better purposes. Now that you have an idea of the things that could be slowing you down in your endeavors, it's time to learn how to get pat them and boost your skills with some methods that can help take you further than you thought was possible. With the tips in this book, you will see a huge increase in your productivity and even find more time for the things that you enjoy in life.

Preview the Information

Take a few moments when starting a new reading to look over the entire thing. Don't spend the same amount of time on this preview as you would when you are actually reading the material, but make sure you look over all parts of it. This step will help you cut out the fluff and focus more thoroughly on the important information that you are looking for.

Use a Pointer

Because your eyes don't remain fixed in position while you are reading, or really when you are doing anything, it can help to train them to stay more focused. They constantly twitch away from your focal point in an effort to take in more information and then it takes a moment to bring them back and to reorganize your thought process. By using a pointer, you force your eyes to stay in the positions that you are trying to. You don't have to buy anything special; just use your finger to follow the lines of text. Keep in mind that this will slow you down when you first start using this method, however as your eyes become used to it, it will cause a greater increase in your reading rate.

Start Simple

When you are first trying to train yourself to speed read, make sure you work with simpler texts. You don't want to immediately dive into trying to read something like a legal document or a technical manual at a fast pace because this will not only lead to you missing the comprehension of these documents, it will discourage you from your efforts. Pick some light, enjoyable reading when you are practicing so you can keep on track.

Don't Sub-vocalize

As discussed in the previous chapter, many people have learned the bad habit of reading to themselves either out load or in a sub-vocal way. It is essential to stop yourself from doing this in order to increase your rate of reading. While this practice isn't always a bad thing when it comes to comprehension, it's not really a necessary habit and it will continue to slow you down. By using your pointer at a faster rate than you can speak or sub-vocalize, you can keep yourself from doing this and eventually train yourself to omit it from your reading completely.

Control is More Important

When you have material that you are reading for a purpose, the most important factor is to understand what you are taking in. This means that you still want to be able to do it as quickly as possible, but you also want to retain the knowledge that you get. Learn to control the speed that you read at, by prioritizing the sections during your preview. You will be able to go very quickly, even skimming, through many portions, but slow yourself down when you get to the more difficult parts so that you can fully comprehend them. Remember, you can always make up the pace that you lost in the easier portions.

Remove Distractions

It may become less important when you become more accustomed to reading at a faster pace, but when you are fist trying to get there, make sure that you are in a quiet, peaceful area. It's easy to get distracted from what you are doing, especially when the material you are trying to get through isn't the most interesting text. Turn off the music or the television and ensure that you are reading in a well-lit place to best facilitate what you are trying to achieve.

Practice Makes Perfect

No matter how many of the other tips you use, if you don't practice your skills, then they won't get any better. The most important thing that you can do to improve your speed reading skills is to read more. In this case, practicing doesn't mean just reading every day; it means consciously pushing the limits of your capabilities every day. Use the pointer and the other tips laid out and try to get your speed up as you practice. This can best be done by specifically setting some time aside for this activity and making an effort to improve your skills.

Chapter 8: The 'Where' Of NLP

High Stress Jobs:

Some professions such as medical legal, security etc. require extreme high levels of energy and effort. Anytime an emergency case pops up, people have to report at all odd hours of the day and always be on their toes. Hence, during downtime, it is important these people working in these sectors maintain a cool peace of mind, as loss of focus on the job can have drastic, disastrous consequences. It is easier to lose focus as the brain is always in a state of over-work and tension.

In such cases, even while the person is resting, the unconscious mind exists in a state of anticipation, and this eventually leads to a mental breakdown among people working in such situations. NLP helps to avoid such undesirable situations by letting people take control of their own minds. It helps in dealing with their routine tasks in a much smoother way, hence enabling them to coordinate their personal and professional lives better.

Planning Jobs:

Jobs such as business, marketing and engineering which require a lot of planning, reap a lot of benefits by employing NLP trained minds. Having a vision and working towards it, with fortitude, is the prerequisite for NLP, thus it proves helpful to the people working in these fields, as it is also a job requirement in such professions. Long term projects require responsible decision making, which is one of the quality developed by NLP.

Creative Jobs:

The basic foundation of NLP is to break preconceived notions thereby making the mind more flexible. This quality comes in handy when the person is employed in a field requiring creative expertise, like that of a painter, writer or actor. When NLP is practiced, the mind becomes willing to take risks and is also determined to convert these risks into rewards. New ideas emerge automatically when all three levels of the mind have been accessed completely. Additionally, the interpretation of these ideas does not require a lot of effort, as in the case of untrained minds.

Social Life:

As important as personal and professional life can be, a person's social life matters equally in today's world. New people offer opportunities for new experiences and exploring uncharted territories also boosts up our self-esteem. Different people move in different social circles, some large, some not as much. But just having a large social circle does imply that a person is handling it well. It is important to be able to manage one's social circle in the most efficient, yet amiable manner possible, in a way that it interferes neither with one's personal life nor with professional.

A chaotic social life is a bane in disguise of a boon. NLP improves our communication, as it is important to voice our opinions, but not at the cost of belittling the voices of others. The key is to strike a balance between our confidence and humility. NLP trains our mind to recognize and maintain this sense of balance. Also, stereotyping and generalizing are two of the biggest obstacles needed to be overcome while building a healthy social life. NLP imparts the character of open mindedness which helps in the long run while creating a healthy society.

Relationships:

Nowadays, relationships are getting harder to manage, owing to the humdrum of commotion in the human mind, as well as impatience and the tendency to give up displayed by most people. This leads to disastrous cases of estrangement, divorces, separation among families etc. Oftentimes, all communications within a family becomes null, as it only leads to further misunderstandings and divide. NLP adds the much required discipline needed to avoid such conflicts, to our lives, by urging the unconscious mind to interfere and submerge the urge to react aggressively. This can be done with the help of NLP as it increases the speed of functioning of the unconscious mind. It trains the mind to have a say in important matters, recognize the conflict and teaches it to accept that conflict is nothing to fuss over.

When a difference in opinion arises in both parties, a middle ground can be reached through mutual compromise, or at the very least a mutual respect can be introduced. Thus, mountains will not be made out of molehills, and estrangement cases can be avoided. With the globalization of world, at some point or the other in life, many couples live in different countries in order to pursue their professional life. With this, infidelity has emerged to be a common issue as people move on quickly and leave behind old relations. NLP trains human nature to not give in to the temptation of a lucrative offer, be it emotional or physical. It raises our conscience so that we don't fall in to the trap of cheating on our partner.

Chapter 9: Strategies to Increase Your Memory Acquisition, Consolidation, and Retention

To improve your memory and retain information fast, you have to work on your memory acquisition, consolidation, and retention abilities: these are the three stages of forming a memory and recalling it.

We will start with going through each of these stages so you gain a better understanding of each and then discuss strategies you can use to improve your ability to learn things and retain them.

Memory Acquisition

To remember any piece of information, you need to learn it first. Learning information (what we call information **acquisition)** is the first stage of memory formation. As you try to learn something, the brain first turns that particular information into temporary neural pathways and that information becomes a component of your short-term memory since this memory has just formed. Most of the information in the short-term memory fade away with time but memories effectively encoded in your brain, those that you pay full attention to and those that you recall repeatedly, remain active for long.

For any short-term memory to convert into a long-term one, it must effectively encode into your brain. Usually, you find it difficult to recall something because you failed to encode that information into your brain. Hence, to improve your cognition, working on memory acquisition is as important as retaining it.

Memory Consolidation

After acquiring a certain piece of information, you need to consolidate that memory so you can effectively recall it when needed. **Consolidating** information is the second step of the process. To recall any information, the brain needs to have converted that information into long-term memory.

You can recall things stored in your long-term memory since the brain periodically filters information stored in your short-term memory. This is important so your mind does not overflow with clutter from unnecessary and meaningless information and can focus better on what is important.

Coming back to memory consolidation, to turn any information into long-term memory, there must be reinforcement of the neuronal pathways related that information. Memory consolidation is the process through which the strengthening of a certain neuronal pathway happens.

Many factors play a role in memory consolidation. Of these factors, the two important ones are connection of new information with memories stored in your long-term memory, and the emotional influence of that new information. If a certain piece of information is connected to any already formed memory and strongly affects you emotionally, you are likely to remember it for good because its neuronal pathways become strong in your brain. Once a certain memory forms and consolidates, you can retrieve it from your long-term memory.

Memory Retrieval and Retention

Retrieval is the third step of the process and is precisely the step you need to execute to retain any information. The retrieval of different pieces of information takes different times. Usually, the more familiar you are with a certain piece of information and the more you recall it, the quicker you will retrieve that information.

For instance, if you memorize the order of elements in the periodic table several times daily, it will take you a few seconds to retrieve that information from your long-term memory. It may take someone else probably 20 or more minutes to recall that same order and those who are yet to memorize that information or have done it a few times only may take ages to recall that pattern.

Moreover, since neuronal activation patterns of memories linked to each other overlap, often you recall something similar when trying to remember specific information. For example, if you are trying to recall the name of Will Smith's first movie, you may keep remembering the name of his current hit since the neuronal pathways of the two pieces of information overlap.

To improve your cognition and become adept at retaining information, you need to improve your ability to acquire new information, consolidate it, and then retain it. Strong memory acquisition helps you encode information successfully in your brain; consolidating that information strengthens the neuronal pathways linked to that information and the ability to retrieve information faster ensures you recall an important piece of information on time.

Let us see how you can do all of that:

Strategies to Improve Your Ability to Learn Things and Retain Them

The following strategies improve your ability to acquire, consolidate, and retain information.

Mnemonic Devices

These popular and commonly used tools sharpen your memory by allowing you to consolidate even the toughest of information. Mnemonic memory improvement technique helps you easily memorize information by helping you associate the respective information with images, phrases, words, and sentences.

Below are a few effective mnemonic devices you can use to strengthen the neuronal activity of any important information you have learnt so you recall it whenever needed.

Form Acronyms

Acronyms are shortcuts you can use to memorize difficult strings of information. In this strategy, you pick the initials of any word or phrase you want to memorize and organize them in a manner to form a catchy name or word you can easily memorize. For example, students learn how to memorize the names of the 5 Great Lakes: **H**uron, **O**ntario, **M**ichigan, **E**rie and **S**uperior using the acronym HOMES.

Another mnemonic tool closely linked to acronym is acrostic. Acrostic is a catchy phrase you create to memorize a short word, piece of information, or series of information. For instance, most people memorize the notes on the bass staff 'ACEG' with the help of the acrostic 'all cows eat grass.'

Each time you have a difficult or big chunk of information to memorize, organize it in the manner you want to learn it in. Next, take out the initials of each word to build a striking acrostic or acronym and then chant it repeatedly.

Speak it aloud along with its actual meaning at least 50 times and then write it down on several post-its. Put those up at different places of your house or workplace so you go through it quickly each time you come across it. This helps you consolidate the information you fed into your short-term memory, which helps turn that memory into a long-term one. As you repeat that mnemonic frequently, it becomes easier for you to recall it on time.

Use Imagery

Visual imagery is an effective mnemonic strategy you can use to learn the names of places, people, and anything else that is seemingly difficult to learn. To use it, you have to associate the information you wish to learn with different creative images that are attractive to you.

For instance, if you keep forgetting that your boss **'Shauna'** likes her coffee with two cubes of sugar and a teaspoon of milk, imagine your boss swimming in a pool of black coffee with two sugar cubes around her and a teaspoon of milk in her mouth. While this is hilarious and may seem silly, just imagine this scenario for a minute and you will never forget this information again. Each time you have to memorize something important and tricky, try this technique and you will never have trouble recalling that information again.

Model Mnemonic

Model mnemonic is a great tool you can use to memorize difficult processes related to chemistry, biology, botany, mathematics, physics, and several other subjects. You can also use it to memorize detailed information related to your business or the different projects you are handling for the organization you work in or your own company.

To use a model mnemonic, you need to represent the information you want to learn in the form of a chart, pyramid, circular sequence model, 5-box sequence, pie chart, graph, or in any other model that allows you easier memorization of the information. For instance, if you turn the Krebs Cycle into a circular sequence model and divide it into quarters and work on learning one quarter at a time and then move on to the next, you will easily memorize and retain the entire process.

Use these mnemonic tools to imbed difficult pieces of information into your brain so you recall it quickly. Another great way to do the same is the mental snapshot strategy.

Mental Snapshot Strategy

This is a fantastic approach you can use to memorize the faces and names of people and recall their names whenever you want without going through a series of "hmms" or "I'm sorry I forgot your name" every time you meet someone you have met before and someone you wish to build a long-term relationship with. People hate it when you cannot recognize them or remember their name especially if you have met a few times before. Such forgetfulness casts a bad impression and the person on the other end is likely to ignore you the next time you approach.

To ensure this does not happen to you and you do not lose an opportunity to build good contacts, use the mental snapshot approach to memorize and recall names, faces, and other important information associated to your contacts. To practice it, do the following:

Whenever you meet someone you wish to meet again, build good rapport with, and turn into your social contact, quickly snap a shot of his/her face. Choose any of that person's distinct facial feature and snap it: we call this a 'face snap.' For instance, if you meet someone with a big nose, focus on the big nose and take a snapshot of his face.

Next, create a name snap of that person. Names fall into two categories: those with a meaning that arouses a visual image and those that do not evoke any specific visual image. For instance, Brown, Bishop, Long, White, Charlie, and Dick are names that evoke visual images and have a specific meaning. I have a friend called 'Mason White.' To memorize his name the first time we met, I imagined a mason working on a completely white building. That is how I easily remembered his name after forgetting it twice. To make someone's name snap, first figure out the category to which her/his name belongs. If her name evokes an image, use it to create a name snap. If not, use syllables in her name to build a viable image. For example, to memorize the name 'Sandy Clarks,' imagine Clark Kent (Superman) relaxing on a sandy beach.

In the end, join the name snap to the face snap using imagery that amalgamates both snapshots. For example, a colleague of mine 'Will Crawford' with big, brown eyes. My face snap of him is his beautiful, brown eyes and his name snap is Will Smith dancing with Cindy Crawford. When I join these snaps together, I imagine Will Smith and Cindy Crawford praising my colleague's gorgeous, brown eyes.

Use this fun, creative approach to memorize the names and faces of people and easily build good contacts.

Do Something Creative and Enjoyable

In addition to doing the above, incorporate a creative and enjoyable activity into your routine and habitually do it. Why is this important? A Study conducted by researchers at the Michigan State University proved that those who take part in creative activities such as arts and crafts have better cognition and are more likely to end up living a more empowered life when compared to those who fail to engage in creative activities.

Creative activities give you a fresh break from your routine activities, challenge you to think outside the box and do something enjoyable. This sharpens your cognition, thus allowing you to think better, acquire and consolidate information faster, and retrieve it quickly.

To benefit from this approach, do something creative daily. You could enroll in an arts program or class, learn to play an instrument or build something using wood, or make DIY creations at home. If you don't think you have the time or money for a class try coloring. It is easier than drawing because all you have to do is fill in the spaces that are already there, but it still requires creativity to choose colors and coloring techniques. Coloring books for adults are widely available and you can find some inexpensive and unique coloring books published by Mindful Coloring Books. You do not need to be amazing at any of this: you just need to do it for fun and for the sake of making yourself think innovatively. Once you do any creative activity a few times, you will start enjoying it and are likely to stick to it for good.

Chapter 10: Benefits of Accelerated Learning

Accelerated learning offers students a way to learn quickly and efficiently, both in the classroom and on their own. Nothing can get you to learn instantaneously, but once you understand the techniques you can use to speed up the learning process, you can use them every day.

In this chapter, I'll explain the key benefits of accelerated learning to help you understand what you can gain by using the techniques in this book.

Better Recall

Human memory can be a fickle thing. Sometimes we recall information easily, and other times it can be a real struggle.

Your ability to recall information at will is closely tied to how you learn it. Any time you pick up new information, it must go first to your short-term memory, and from there, to long-term memory.

The way you study and how you learn both play a role in how easy it is for you to recall information. Accelerated learning provides you with techniques to help you focus and to build the kind of strong neural connections that make it easy for you to remember information when you need to do so.

Less Wasted Time

Many students waste time when they study. They get distracted, they lose their train of thought, and as a result, they end up taking far longer than necessary to commit new information to memory.

The techniques of accelerated learning can change that. Because they minimize procrastination and improve focus, accelerated learning can help you cut to the chase. You won't waste time because you won't need to.

Less Procrastination

Procrastination is a common problem for students who struggle. Learning feels difficult and so they seek out other things to do to avoid it. The problem, of course, is that many of us fall into harmful patterns where procrastination becomes second nature. We push everything until the last minute – and we may even tell ourselves that we work better under pressure to justify our actions.

Accelerated learning helps eliminate procrastination by making the learning process efficient and easy.

Better Grades

Getting below-average grades turns into a vicious cycle for some students. Since a student's sense of self-worth can be closely tied to their grades, it's hardly surprising that a poor performance in school can become a real self-esteem problem.

Accelerated learning increases recall and teaches students how to learn. Instead of simply throwing them into a classroom, it helps students discipline themselves and actively seek out the information they need to perform well in class.

More Success

People who learn easily tend to be successful. Their ability to absorb new information and learn new skills sets them up for success in every area of life.

Accelerated learning demystifies the learning process and helps students embrace the classroom as a friendly and welcoming place. They learn techniques that help them succeed in school – and later in life, they will be able to apply the same techniques to their work.

Success means different things to different people, but accelerated learning can help you find your success – no matter what you do.

Now that you understand the benefits of accelerated learning, let's move on. Next up, I'll share some information about how to focus on your studies and avoid distractions.

Chapter 11: Additional Learning Techniques

Name your favorite movie. Is it Casablanca or Superman or something else?

If you look back and dissect your viewing experience of this movie - whether it's an action movie, thriller or a romantic comedy - you will realize that your total experience is made up of a number of bits and pieces. The story, the performances, the dialogue, the music, the setting, the action and the atmosphere are just some of the more important bits and pieces. Together, these pieces fit in to make a grand picture.

This is true of your memory also.

Your learning and recall processes make use of auditory, visual, tactile, kinesthetic, organizational and cognitive processes to take in data. Your setting, the atmosphere and the kind of life you lead are some of the other crucial factors that influence your learning process. So you see, a number of bits and pieces make up your learning experience.

Your brain is truly an amazing machine because it improves with use. It is a little busybody that is always trying to add new bits and pieces to your learning process. As you develop more and more methods for learning, your ability to take in data increases by leaps and bounds.

For instance, a student who starts using the link or the association method for learning may find it difficult to make the necessary links, at first. However, if he sticks with it, he will soon start linking and associating automatically. His brain adapts itself to this new method of learning.

Supplemental learning methods are often suggested in accelerated learning classes because they allow your brain to develop more methods of learning. With every new skill that is learnt, the brain develops further by .2 – .8% (if you think that's too little, you might want to remember that Einstein is supposed to have used up only 12% of his brain power!).

Supplemental learning is above all beneficial for people who have left their school learning days far behind. When you reach that stage, you are no longer comfortable with rote-learning. The time factor is also important when you have to learn pages of data for the weekend meeting or for the big presentation scheduled for next week.

In these circumstances, the more versatile your brain the faster will it learn. Supplemental learning techniques increase the osmotic capacity of your mind, making it sharper and more fertile. In due course, your brain becomes primed for learning.

Some of the most common supplemental learning techniques are:

1. Set your objectives: How many times have you heard children say 'I'm just dumb, I just don't know anything about that'? Fact is, if you were to question them on the topic, you would surprise them with how much they knew. Many people are blissfully unaware of what they already know and what they **need** to know.

Objective-setting is an important part of the accelerated learning techniques. Determine what you know, figure out what you don't know and then learn what you need to know. This simple step can save you a lot of time.

2. Read voraciously: Reading up more on a particular topic helps you get the breadth of the topics covered. Your brain works to make links and cross references. A seemingly trivial example or law might well be a 'light-bulb' moment that finally clarifies a concept. This is an area where your speed reading skills can help you tremendously.

3. Learn a new language: Cross-pollinating your interests can really help you speed up your learning process. Learning a new language adds a new perspective and gives you the ability to cross-pollinate ideas and concepts. Sometimes, reading a book in its original language exposes you to nuances that are often lost in translation.

4. Think holistically: This is an important part of your learning process. Try to see the bigger picture and determine how

everything adds up to form a whole.
5. Over stimulation: In traditional learning classes, teachers are almost afraid of throwing too much at their students at once. According to the theory of accelerated learning, the human brain can assimilate almost 80% more information than what we assume. Bombarding the brain with information through long texts, dramatization, visualization and the like can be quite useful because a lot of data is taken in automatically.
6. Equip yourself with all the necessary tools: As learning becomes a scientifically backed activity, there is a flood of study tools and kits in the market. Consider using online tools, learning software and Web applications to speed up your learning process.

Chapter 5.0 Recap:

• Supplementary learning techniques stimulate your brain to make use of all its resources.
• Set your goals before you begin.

- Speed read as much data as you can.
- Think   holistically.
- Over stimulate so that the amount of data   you   take   in   is   more.

Chapter   5.1:   Learn   Languages   By Combining Techniques

How many languages do you know? (Hint: the answer to this question is directly related to how smart you are!)

According to modern research, people who know more than 2 languages have brains that are more developed than people who know only one language. Scientists believe that learning a new language can actually increase the gray matter in the brain. Research suggests that even being bilingual has its benefits: it boosts your problem solving skills and delays cognitive decline as you age. Now you know why those language classes are so important.

Learning a foreign language is no piece of cake. Anybody who has tried it knows how difficult it is to learn a new language using traditional learning methods. Even after all the hard work, retention rates are quite poor unless you keep revising the new language consistently.

However, there are certain study techniques that can make your language study more efficient and less time-consuming. The icing on the cake is that these study techniques guarantee you **30-50%** less study time with **70-80%** more data recall **even without further revision**.

The two main aspects of language study are:

• Vocabulary learning

• Practicing

Vocabulary:
Learning a new vocabulary is a daunting task. Imagine having to memorize words that sound funny and make no sense to you! As far as you are concerned, the French word for 'notebook' could be 'cahier', 'pierre' or 'abcd..'. It really doesn't matter because you do not have

any inner springboard against which you could test the correctness of this new knowledge.

So, how can you learn vocabulary? Traditionally, students learned new words and phrases through repetitive reading and writing. The process was quite simple: say a word in the foreign language and then repeat it in your own language.

The problem with this process is that it is tedious, boring and time-consuming. Worse still, students tend to lose more than 40% of what they learn **immediately**.

In order to learn foreign words quickly, you have to make use of a mechanism that will form associations between foreign words and your own language **fairly quickly**. Traditional learning methods use repetition (which is boring and tiresome) as the basis of this link formation. But by now, you would have realized that with accelerated learning techniques, you have a number of faster and more effective association methods at your disposal.

Using Mnemonics to learn vocabulary:

The LinkWord system: Remember the association method we talked about earlier, where you use associations to link ideas? To learn vocabulary fairly quickly, you can use a simple extension of the association technique.

Use images to link a foreign word with words in your language.

To take the earlier example of notebook or 'cahier' in French, you can easily see that the word 'cahier' closely resembles 'cashier'.

Cahier

So picture a cashier sitting at his desk with

a pile of money working with his accounting **notebook**! You are now assisting your brain to make a connection between 'Cahier', 'Cashier' and 'Notebook'.

Here are some more examples to get you going on the idea:

• The French word for rug or carpet is 'Tapis'. Imagine buying a carpet that has a real tap dripping in its center – with real water that is being sucked back in! (In true Harry Potter fashion)
• The French word for horse is 'Cheval'. Doesn't that word sound like 'Shovel'? Imagine a horse shoveling snow from you front yard using a platinum shovel!

This technique is called the 'LinkWord' technique and it was formalized by Dr. Gruneberg, who used it to assist students to learn German. According to proponents, the 'LinkWord' system will help you learn the basic vocabulary of any language in just 10 hours!

The Loci Technique: Also known as the Roman Room Technique, this is an ancient and effective method for remembering information when the exact structure of the information is not important. It has now evolved to become one of the most powerful Mnemonic systems used to learn languages.

To begin with, imagine a room that you are very familiar with. Your sitting room, office or library is good enough. Next, think about the objects in the room. Using images associate the words you want to remember with the objects in the room.

When it is time to recall the information, simply take a tour around the room in your mind visualizing the object and image you have formed. You can add new information by opening the door of this room and entering other rooms to make use of the objects there.

If you are more familiar with landscapes, gardens, parks or a town, you can use these settings instead of the room.

For instance, think about your library. As you enter the library, there is a big desk. Sitting at the desk with his legs on it is the cashier and his pile of money. Imagine the cashier writing his accounts into his notebook as you enter the room. Just as you approach the cashier, you walk on a beautifully crafted carpet which has a running tap in the middle. And so it goes on...

A simple way to keep remembering the associations you have formed (if you forget the associations, you've had it) is to make Flash cards, with the foreign word on one side and the native word on the other. As you remember each word, try to visualize the associated images so that the associations become strongly embedded in   your   mind.
Some more shortcuts:

Pattern spotting is an easy way to develop that king-sized vocabulary. For instance, suppose you were learning Spanish. As a beginner, what if you were told that every word ending in 'tion' in English ends with 'ción' in Spanish? You would have immediate access to thousands of words at one stroke!

Another technique is to look for similarities between two languages – one that you know and the other that you aim to learn. For instance, the French word for cherries is 'Cerises' and for letter is 'lettre'. There may be similarities in pronunciation, spelling or just the meaning. It does not matter what the similarity is so long as you spot it.

Many languages categorize words into the male and female genders. To make your life difficult, what is male in German may be female in French and neutral in English! To help you with this, imagine all the male words linked to a male person. For instance, Horse or "cheval' is male in French. So, picture a boy sitting on top of the horse while it shovels the snow.

Baroque music can help you learn foreign languages. Dr Lazanov used certain pieces of baroque music to teach German to his students. His experiment conclusively showed that foreign languages can be learned 85-90% more efficiently in only 30 days by using baroque pieces of music. What is most interesting is that students who used this technique retained more than **90% of what they learnt** even after 4 years – without any revision!

Language   Practice: Learning vocabulary is only one part of the language learning process, although it is the meatiest part. Your language learning does not stop there. What about grammar and pronunciation?

Of course, your best option is to use the language whenever and wherever you can. As they say 'when in Rome, do as Romans do' so it's true 'when you want to learn Spanish, go where Spaniards live'.

Learning from native speakers enables you to use language-specific intonation, learn grammar rules easily and practice native pronunciation methodology. Therefore it should be a priority to listen to the foreign language as much as possible. However, it's not always possible to have direct access to native speakers.

That is where technology can help you.

• Invest in some audio resources, CDs or language tapes.

• Listen to radio and watch television running programs in the language of your choice.

• Listen to music in the language you want to learn. You may not understand the words, but you will pick them up subconsciously.

• Watch movies in the foreign language. That way, some words can be picked up easily (especially 'emotional' words and words that you'd normally not use in polite conversation).

As you go through the techniques descried here, you may feel that some of them are long-winded and difficult. Yes, these techniques require time, energy and patience to develop. But over a period of time using these techniques will cut your study time by more than half! So, it is well worth investing some time and effort into getting used to these alternative strategies for learning.

At the end of the day, these techniques are only a 'crutch' to your actual learning process. Once you use a word a couple of times, you will automatically know that 'cahier' means notebook in French – if you don't   know   it   already!

Chapter 5.1 Recap:

• The two fundamental parts of language learning are: Vocabulary learning and Practicing.
• Traditional learning techniques depend on repetitive reading and writing to master   vocabulary.
• To learn much faster and to retain more, you have to use your entire brain while learning.
• You can master vocabulary 45% faster by using the 'LinkWord' technique and the Loci   method.
• You can make use of Flash cards to remember and revise the new words you

have   learnt.
• Pattern   spotting   and   working   out
similarities can help you learn new words
faster.

• To improve your language skills, listen to
the foreign language as much as you can.

• Use radio, TV, movies, Audio tapes, CDs
and music to enhance and speed up your
learning process.

Chapter 12: How to Improve Memory and Concentration - The Results Will Amaze You!

How frequently have you overlooked very similar things again and again? It appears as though you neglect to accomplish something or lose very identical jobs every week. Wouldn't it be pleasant when you could recollect where you put your eyeglasses or the keys to the vehicle? Shy of placing them in the same spot unfailingly, there ought to be different manners by which you can figure out how to improve memory and focus. This part will talk about a couple of the things that should be possible to enable you to improve your absent-minded ways.

Focus

Fixation and memory are relatively comparative when you consider it. If you recall the majority of the many occasions that you have overlooked where you left your eyeglasses, you may discover that they were not lost since you forgot where you put them, but since you were not focusing on where you left them. A ton of times, individuals make a halfhearted effort of their ordinary assignments without concentrating on what they are doing. If you are acquainted with doing things likewise again and again consistently, for example, perusing and after that taking your eyeglasses off, your psyche mostly dominates and makes a cursory effort for you.

Sooner or later, during this procedure, you are not focusing on what you are doing. Along these lines, losing your glasses cannot be accused of your memory. Consider the rationale. How might you remember something when you were not by any stretch of the imagination focusing around then? One of the main things that you should, when you like to figure out how to improve memory and fixation, is to focus on what you are doing. When this is done, you can proceed onward to different things that will viably utilize the intensity of your mind, yet you must initially figure out how to appropriately deal with it.

Keep Your Brain Fit

Much the same as the remainder of your body, your cerebrum likewise needs to stay fit and sound to work appropriately. This is a significant standard guideline that you should recall whether you wish to figure out how to improve memory and focus. Coming up next are only a couple of the things that you should consider when you are attempting to improve both your mind and fixation:

Exercise Your Mind-Your cerebrum is a muscle that necessities practice to work appropriately. Without a doubt, it is utilized once a day for the more significant part of your everyday undertakings. However, it likewise must be strenuously practiced for it to work taking care of business. For instance, doing straightforward fun and simple assignments, for example, comprehending crossword riddles can assist you with keeping your cerebrum getting it done.

Push your mind to the maximum with regards to your reasoning abilities. The additional push is the thing that you ought to do once a day if you need to figure out how to improve memory and fixation genuinely.

Diminish Stress-Find approaches to lessen your feelings of anxiety. The cerebrum cannot work appropriately when it is exhausted because of your raised feelings of anxiety. In any case, before you can address your issues of not having the option to think and improve your memory, discover what is causing your pressure. Keep in mind that one of the fundamental things that enhance your capacity to figure out how to improve memory and fixation is your capacity to center and focus on what you are doing. If your feelings of anxiety are raised, there is something that is causing a great deal of diversion in your life. Until you deal with circumstances, for example, this, you won't be able to concentrate on different parts of your life, which will consistently forget about you pushed and baffled. Diminishing your feelings of anxiety, and you will find that odds of figuring out how to improve memory and focus will likewise improve.

Unwind Your mind won't perform taking care of business if you are worried and tired constantly. You should discover approaches to unwind. This may be something as straightforward as expanding the measure of time doing fun things that you like to do, for example, investing energy with your family, practicing or shopping. Fundamentally, discovering approaches to build your unwinding time will help in your journey of figuring out how to improve memory and focus.

Diet and Exercise-Contrary to conviction, yet a sound personality and body go close by. Most occasions, when one is undesirable, the other will unquestionably endure also. If you need to figure out how to improve memory and fixation, at that point, you will need to deal with both your body and psyche. Your psyche cannot stay solid if your body is unbalanced. Ensure that you get enough exercise during the day. The cerebrum is just one of the muscles that your body has. You should ensure that different muscles in your body are likewise appropriately worked out.

Notwithstanding exercise, ensure that your body gets the best possible measure of rest and sustenance. The absence of rest will make you feel drowsy, which will, without a doubt, negatively affect your capacity to retain things or concentrate. Eating the off-base sorts of nourishments can likewise make your body respond negatively. Taking specific herbal enhancements, for example, Ginkgo Biloba and rosemary have been connected to improving memory and making you increasingly alert.

Memory Games-Making utilization of memory amusements is an astounding method to enable you to figure out how to improve memory and focus. This can be something as straightforward as utilizing certain traps to recall a person's name. For example, when meeting new individuals, if you imagine that you will experience serious difficulties recollecting that person's name, partner this new person with something that you know about. For instance, does this new person help you to remember something about another person? This would be a brilliant method to review their name later on. Consider something natural that you can connect them with later on.

By and extensive figuring out how to improve memory and fixation ought to be an essential undertaking when you pursue the tips in this part. Keep in mind that before you can recall something, you need to focus on what you are doing. Evacuate the majority of the diversions that ruin your capacity to concentrate on what you ought to do. Figure out how to focus and appropriately deal with your mind. These are the main things that will assist you in learning how to improve your memory and fixation.

Step by step instructions to Improve Memory Recall With Meditation

A lot of items and administrations - drugs or mental medicines - are given to help improve memory review with various impacts. Anybody can see the outcomes with straightforward research of the different medical diaries printed on the web. Pause for a minute to consider this, our progenitors did not have the extravagance or the methods for the created medicines of present occasions, or the medications made today. So if they can improve memory review without anyone else with contemplation systems, for what reason right?

Reflection isn't only exclusively situated in one thing like in prior occasions when they depended on Religious convictions. To pick up capability in thinking, certain practices can be over and overdone. It very well may be difficult for individuals to pick up a fundamental comprehension of how contemplation works, when these individuals cannot appreciate how it capacities, at that point, what more when they need to try it.

Here is a snappy once-over of specific procedures that still show their capacity to be both amazing and viable:

1. Breathing Exercises

This is about the calming rhythm of your body. The clamors a body makes as it takes in and out acts as a basic metronome. The mind at that point unwinds just as conveying more oxygen to the cerebrum and the entire body.

2. Clear Your Mind

A quick-paced world is brimming with duties that cannot be disregarded. There are diversions that we experience, for example, arbitrary contemplations. Commotions or physical requests can likewise go about as outside interruptions.

Just exhausting your brain requires a suspension of faith in outer powers, for example, duties and clamors for at any rate 60 minutes. An hour is sufficient to procure an essential reflective stage.

3. Quiet and Stillness

Individuals basically cannot achieve a meditative state amidst a storm. Commotions and physical requests can be evaded by just heading off to a confined region. Once there, you can do your reflection procedure in harmony.

Improving Memory Retention Through Healthy Habits

Numerous individuals expect that incredible memory is something that usually happens. The facts confirm that a few people may often hold sure musings and can recall data simpler than others. Improving memory maintenance through sound propensities can regularly exceed expectations you to a "skilled" person level in next to zero time by any means.

If you weren't brought into the world with an extraordinary memory, that is okay. I wasn't either. Nowadays, after some training, it's turned out to be much simpler to hold more significant and more prominent measures of data. Possibly you need to have the option to recall straightforward things, for example, where you left your keys, or what bills you have to get paid when. Whatever your explanations behind improving memory maintenance are, these solid propensities will make it much more straightforward.

Exercise

Practice does ponder for your memory. All together for your cerebrum to hold data, it must be in a healthy state. Not to sound prosaism, however being in a solid perspective can mean various things. Ordinary exercise will expand bloodstream and oxygen immersion inside the cerebrum. This will generally prompt improved memory and a general prosperity perspective.

Exercise is incredible for some reasons, and however, concerning the subject of memory, it's imperatively significant. You don't need to work yourself out to weariness, yet a decent 15-20 minutes of cardiovascular exercise will help immensely.

Sufficient Sleep

Keeping up a sound rest example is crucially significant for improving memory maintenance. I wince each time I consider how often I pulled overnighters concentrating for school tests. I can recollect experiencing parts and sections of science and brain research books attempting to pack as much as I could before I went in for the test. I would typically leave an hour or two and no more of rest.

By one way or another, I generally figured out how to do "okay," yet the foggy head I would understanding during the test was unquestionably a piece of information that I would improve a tad of rest.

This applies to regular daily existence too. When you have poor memory, and you feel tired during the day, you could be denying your body and brain of very much required rest. Some of the time 30 minutes to an hour is all you have to get your mind the measure of rest it needs to improve your memory.

Diet

Frequently neglected, your eating regimen can contribute intensely to improving memory maintenance. I won't haul out a long section about how you ought to have one or the other concerning your eating regimen. Anyway, it's imperative to keep your eating routine adjusted.

Have you at any point conversed with somebody that is slimming down in-your-face? A well-known occurrence is reviewed when I endeavored to complete a "low carb" diet. Numerous individuals that deny themselves of specific supplements, protein, starches, or some other piece of a sound and adjusted eating regimen regularly get an overcast personality. Ask anybody that is ever effectively been on a low carb diet for a not too bad measure of time.

This subject can go off digression in all respects effectively so I'll bring it back in and recommend that you keep your eating regimen offset and enhanced with your ordinary nutrient stack.

Following these tips for improving memory maintenance will get you in good shape for recollecting every one of the things you never figured you could! Trust me, and it's much simpler to remember pretty much anything when your body and psyche are sound.

Memory Improvement Supplements

This previous couple of years, sustenance enhancements have been very prevalent as a result of its capacity to improve your general wellbeing and execution, particularly memory improvement. These memory improvement enhancements are delivered utilizing the most normally - happening fixings that have been used by individuals for different purposes for hundreds and thousands of years. When you need to recognize what are these memory improvement supplements that would enable you to help your memory execution, you have unquestionably gone to the perfect spot. I have quite recently the adequate measure of data that would make you go. You don't need to go somewhere else, looking for it on any place you would consider looking through it, sparing you the cerebral pain and the inconvenience that it may cause you only for looking through it yourself. That is without a doubt valid for there are numerous fake sources on the web that may give you poor outcomes instead of the results that are proposed for you by the veritable memory improvement enhancements and items. So why hazard it? We guarantee that when you have wrapped up this article, you would have a clear thought and you would likewise have different choices to browse to improve your memory. So all you need to do presently is no other than: read this cracking article, for the wellbeing of God!

We should get serious. These are the different memory improvement supplements that you could take. Mind you, these are inquired about and demonstrated enhancements, none of these are inadequate so delve in.

Gingko Balboa - this is maybe the most intense enhancement with regards to memory upgrade. It thoroughly causes you to keep up ordinary blood dissemination, particularly on the cerebrum, permitting consistent memory capacities. This is because of the way that blood resembles a vehicle or a taxi inside your veins; it transports stuff, particularly oxygen to your mind so the legitimate course would support you.

Rosemary - no, I'm not discussing your auntie. I'm talking about a similar fixing that you use for flavor in your cooking. These can be broadly found in the Mediterranean, much more happening than grass. The best thing about rosemary (the herb, not your auntie.) is that it legitimately influences and improves your mind capacities. What I mean about direct is that it doesn't do whatever else like improving blood flow and stuff, it straightforwardly enhances your mind.

Green Tea - this is one of the most widely recognized enhancements and tea drink on the planet at present. It has bunches of advantages, and one of them is, correct, you got it, memory upgrade. It additionally fixes a wide range of illnesses and maladies. Drink this together with dark tea, and you'll get all out wellbeing and memory benefits, ensured.

There are things that you ought to consider before you take this memory improvement enhancement like addicts. Initially, you should confide in specific brands because not all providers can be believed; some are spiked with added substances to cause it to show up bounty so better watch out for that.

What Supplements to Take For Memory Improvement?

In recent years, natural supplements have picked up a great deal of prevalence in improving wellbeing and generally speaking prosperity. Naturally, you can likewise discover supplements gainful for your memory improvement.

Such supplements are created from happening natural substances, and individuals have been utilizing them in various ways for hundreds and possibly a large number of years.

Useful impact of natural supplements on by and broad wellbeing has been all around demonstrated by time and a considerable number of clients.

1) Gingko Biloba Extract is, by all accounts, the supplement that has the best effect on memory improvement. The impact that Ginkgo Biloba has on a body is that it improves the blood course all through your body just as your cerebrum.

Blood is, in addition to other things, an oxygen transportation apparatus for your body, and when your mind has standard, relentless oxygen supply, it works much better.

On the present market, you can discover many various brands offering Ginkgo Biloba Extract. What's more, they all declare that their item is the best. I would recommend you keep with the outstanding, reputable producers.

2) Rosemary is additionally one of the supplements. Rosemary is often utilized as zest, and if you visit the Mediterranean, you can discover it at every progression developing wild.

Mediterranean eating routine is, with the proposal of WHO, THE best eating regimen you can have. As a homegrown supplement, Rosemary's impact is intriguing such that it appears to invigorate the mind capacities legitimately.

This is an incredible advantage for memory improvement. Likewise, with Ginkgo Biloba, you can discover several names available so stick with the ones you know and trust.

3) Green tea - typically a large portion of natural supplements gainful for memory

improvement help with your general wellbeing condition too. A good case of this is green tea.

Green tea has in the course of the most recent ten years rose as natural assistance in restoring numerous afflictions and medical issues. Green tea alongside the Black tea is accepted to affect cerebrum capacities helpfully and whenever devoured in moderate portions seems, by all accounts, to be valuable for memory improvement.

4) Ginseng is additionally related to memory improvement. All the time associated with noteworthy energy improvement just as in general body rejuvenation, Ginseng moreover appears to affect memory improved significantly.

Similarly, as with the Ginkgo Biloba and Rosemary keep with the marks you know and trust.

For those of you who have quite recently started to feel memory misfortune signs, likely on account of pressure or age, natural supplements can be the best fix just as aversion for this issue.

Natural memory promoters have fewer reactions than standard memory improvement prescription just as the constructive outcome on your general wellbeing condition.

Step by step instructions to Increase Memory Power - Tips To Boost Your Brain Power

Figuring out how to build memory power can be a baffling procedure for some individuals. Some vibe that individuals, when all is said in done either, have a good memory or don't. Albeit specific individuals do have an inborn capacity to adapt quicker, or hold information, the mind is much the same as a muscle that can be fortified utilizing strategies and activities.

Likely one of the most widely recognized methods for how to expand memory power is by the utilization of mental helpers.

Memory helpers are fundamentally word or picture affiliations which, when contemplated, can help you to remember certain occasions, things, names, and so forth.

Another model is for music understudies who are attempting to figure out how to peruse music. Perhaps you've known about the expression "Every Good Boy Deserves Fudge," or a variety of it. Once more, utilizing the central letters of this mental aide, we can build up the names of the notes on each line of a treble clef — e, G, B, D, and F.

This is the thing that we call a first letter mental aide and can be connected to many circumstances. By working on making your psychiatric aides, you can prepare your cerebrum to search for these quicker, and review them faster.

In the equivalent vain, you can utilize perception methods as methods for how to expand memory control. Once more, this is viewed as a mental aide; however, it makes it so when you think about a specific thing, it will identify with items you wish to recall.

How about we accept learning another dialect, for instance. It tends to be extremely hard to recollect vocabulary, particularly in case you're not in the situation to utilize it every day. Be that as it may, if we use a perception of mental helper, we can prepare our cerebrum to connect pictures with words or expressions.

In Japanese, the expression for "Good Night" is "Oyasuminasai." It sounds such a significant amount of unique about its English partner that it could in all likelihood be hard to recall. In any case, if you somehow managed to consider a picture identified with the expression, for example, a Big full moon on a crisp evening's sky, and afterward think about "oyasuminasai" again and again while as yet envisioning the moon, your mind would perceive that these two relate some way or another. So whenever you attempt to recollect what the Japanese word for

"Good Night" is, you would review the enormous moon, and "oyasuminasai."

Notwithstanding mental helpers, you can utilize practices that expansion your fixation, which will likewise incredibly help you on your journey of how to build memory control.

The most straightforward one you can do is known as the "Light Gazing Exercise." With this activity, you permanently light a typical supper flame and spot it about a manageable distance far from your body in an obscured room. You need it to be at around eye level.

Presently, close your eyes and clear your brain as well as can be expected. When you are prepared, open your eyes and look at the flame without squinting. Attempt and spotlight on the light, however much as could reasonably be expected. When your eyes to begin to water and you want to look, close your eyes and attempt and picture the flame.

In this state, you should attempt to recollect all the little subtleties of the flame. From the outset this will be troublesome as you aren't prepared at this point, so don't be debilitated if the light appears somewhat fluffy in your psyche.

After a couple of minutes, open your eyes again and look at the light. Rehash this procedure for in any event 20 minutes every day. The more you practice, the better your focus, which is a crucial segment when attempting to figure out how to build memory control.

Five Suggestions on How to Increase Memory Power

We need our memory to work in our day by day lives. Without it, we can't recollect realities, what we are doing straightaway or significant occasions that occurred in our lives. Since memory is so substantial for day by day life, what would one be able to do if they are experiencing difficulty with it? The five thoughts beneath can help tell the best way to build memory control.

1. Keep away from Certain Foods

There are a few nourishments that are extraordinary for improving memory. Fish is one of these sustenances. Others incorporate the natural product, high-cocoa content chocolate, vegetables, dairy, and oats. This is because they are low on the glycemic list (GI). Sustenances low on the GI takes more time for your body to separate, so they help keep your memory continually dynamic.

A few kinds of sustenances and beverages do the inverse for memory. These sustenances are on the opposite finish of the GI. While OK with some restraint, liquor, soft drink, white bread, and sugars can diminish memory, so lessening the measure of these sustenances in a single eating routine can build memory.

2. Remain Physically Active

Since you increment your body's bloodstream when you work out, you likewise increment bloodstream in your mind. This can support memory. When you ceaselessly remain dynamic, your cerebrum will as well.

3. Exercise your Mind

Riddles, similar to crosswords and computer game secrets, can improve memory. By "practicing the brain," you can strengthen its exhibition for different errands. Developing aptitudes with riddles proposes improvement in memory and cerebrum work.

4. Use Supplements

Omega 3-unsaturated fats can support memory. They explicitly improve cerebrum capacity, center, and correspondence between synapses. Fish contains these acids, as do fish oil and flaxseed oil supplements. Different supplements for memory are Ginkgo Biloba, folic corrosive, and sage oil.

5. Get Rest

If you get to rest, your memory will work better. Rest and unwinding help your mind work appropriately. Sleeping, contemplation, and breathing activities likewise improve memory.

Chapter 13: Self-regulation

Brain Power

The full potential of the human brain is still unknown. It's an organ that weighs on average around three pounds. Who would believe that it contains up to 100-billion interconnected neurons? Yet, this is how information travels around in our grey matter. It is a powerful organ that can:

· Process Information.

· Process complex images.

· Store Memory.

· Control body movements.

· Deal with toxins and flush them away.
· Keep our heart pumping and our lungs breathing.

And, these are only the basics.

Our perplexing brains are busily zapping away with electrical activity 24 hours a day. What's more, the brain continues to grow. It doesn't get any larger but develops more neurons as we actively learn. Researchers creating Artificial Intelligence (AI) showed that the human brain is 30-times more powerful than the world's fastest computer.

With such power going on inside your head, it does make you wonder what our real potential is.

Okay, back down to earth. In reality, we humans are very curious creatures. Mankind is constantly searching for answers to everything that comes their way. As a species, we have a deep routed curiosity to learn all we can throughout our life span. Psychologists label this as "Mastery." With such a capacity to absorb new information and adapt accordingly, you'd think all be equal to Einstein, yet, it's not that simple, is it? Learning takes effort on our part.

Knowledge doesn't just funnel itself into the brain and absorb into our neural network. We have to identify that new knowledge, and then we have to go through the grueling process of putting it there inside our heads so that we can learn from it. Learning new skills leads to a whole new thinking process of creativity. Who knows where this process ends, or can it be continuous throughout your whole life? Yes, it can. Also as being inquisitive creatures, humans also possess a selfish yearning for praise and reward. Without rewards, we seem to lack motivation. In our industrialized world, we're taught to seek monetary rewards, believing this will lend us a better life. To some extent that is true, money can offer an easier existence. Being rich does not necessarily mean you are content with your lot in life. Excessive amounts of cash are no good if you're not a happy person. Imagine then, if you could combine happiness and have enough money to enjoy the better things of life. Can we create a set of circumstances to help us reach our ultimate goals in life?

That's where our clever brain comes in handy. The quicker we learn new skills, the sooner we gain those rewards. To learn at a faster pace though, we would need to craft the essential skill of focusing. This is where mindset comes into place, but what exactly is a healthy mindset?

Self-discipline

It is not an easy feat, to train your mind to focus. This takes time and commitment. Yet, just like training at the gym for a well-defined sculptured body, you can shape the way your mind thinks too. You can train your mind to focus by using the art of self-discipline.

It sounds too easy, doesn't it? Well, it's not! Self-discipline, or lack of it, can often be the downfall of many projects and personal ambitions.

A weight lifter knows that their body is capable of becoming stronger. The first rule they accept is that of self-discipline as they train. They must practice over and over as they perform difficult repetitive exercises. It is no easy task to build up strength, but that is the only way to reach their target. Healthy food is top of the list, and it takes hard work on their part to find a routine in life that works. Many are successful. Those are the ones who understand what they need to do to achieve their ultimate goal. Those who don't reach that goal have lost their way. They must settle for a lesser path, or go a different way altogether. The latter sounds like the option of the majority of the population. This takes us back to the wonderful organ called the brain. As the body can grow in strength, so too can the brain perform amazing feats.

We know the bodybuilder needs a routine to reach his/her target. That is no different from anyone who wishes to reach extraordinary levels. Many successful people have pushed their boundaries beyond normal limitations. How then does the average person do this?

This is where our journey begins.

Know Yourself

This is the only way you are going to drive yourself beyond your normal capability. Admit your faults, find your strengths and build up a routine that will follow a path to your ultimate goal.

This is where you must take a good look at who you are.

Ask yourself these basic questions:

- Do I eat healthy foods?

- Do I eat too much junk food?
- Do I get enough exercise?

- Do I read enough?

- How good is my concentration span?

How well do I sleep?

These questions cover some basic parts of your very existence. That is where you must begin and then build up the building blocks to success. Call it your preparation level. If you are that person who wishes to be successful, then prepare for the training, it can be done.

Chapter 14: Accelerated Learning: An Overview

You may remember those days in college or high school when you spent your days doing what you wanted, hanging out with who you wanted, and enjoying not having any pressing responsibility to do "right now." If you wanted to go out with friends, you were free to do it, if you wanted to simply spend a lazy day in front of the television you were free to do it.

After all, the terms **due tomorrow? Do tomorrow,** and **Cramming for the exam** didn't seem like procrastination but rather a marvelous technique that released you from having to do any kind of responsible activity until the very last minute.

Now, you may be a kid who was great at taking tests and regardless of how long you gave yourself to get ready you would pass with a good grade. Or, you might be one of those kids who tried with all your might to get a good grade, but in spite of all your hard work, you never could be happy with what you accomplished and therefore you never did try very hard.

In either case, you are likely wondering what accelerated learning is, and how it is going to help you now. The first thing you need to realize is that this is not some cheating form of learning that is going to give you the easy break into the world of knowledge. It's not some magic formula that is going to erase your hand in the process.

No, accelerated learning is a learning technique that is going to change the **way** you learn. It's a learning style that in recent years has gained monumental popularity across the world because it is so easy to implement, and incredibly effective in learning. It really doesn't matter how old you are, what your academic level is, or if you are even trying to learn this style for academic purposes.

Accelerated learning is a crucial tool that helps everyone, in every stage of life, and for every possible subject they are learning.

The accelerated learning style is a style that is built on specific pillars. Though there are variations within these pillars and each person is going to use each pillar differently, the core structure remains the same.

The first pillar in accelerated learning is time – people tend to remember the information at the beginning and the end of a given lecture the best, while overlooking or forgetting much of what was in the middle. With accelerated learning, you learn based on this fact.

The next is overall learning – accelerated learning is a learning style that is broken down into different pieces. Instead of getting bogged down with the fine details of a manuscript, you are going to learn the idea as a whole.

Next, is the pillar of change – many people understand that the definition of insanity is to do the same thing and expect a different outcome, but this just isn't the case.

Think about it, if you have been attempting to learn with the same style in the past, and time and time again you find that you fail, what do you think should change?

All hands on deck; the next pillar is senses – the old school rooms of the past – the ones in which all the students sat and listened as the teacher read some horrifyingly boring piece of literature and expected you to remember it – those days are gone.

Learning requires the full use of your brain, and it's going to require that you use all your senses in order to full grasp what it is you are trying to learn. Sure, you might not have to engage all your senses at the same time, but you are going to have to use touch, speech, smell, hearing and all the rest to fully grasp what you are trying to earn if you wish to learn it for the long term.

Don't forget to have some fun – when you aren't having fun, the only thing you are thinking about is when the activity is going to be over, so you are free to get out and have some fun. With accelerated learning, the process of learning should be hands–on.

It should be something that is fun and rewarding to you (or your child if you are helping your child with this technique.) Who said that learning needed to be boring?

Distributed, concentrated practice is the next pillar – I think by now it is safe to say that we all know that cramming for exams is not the way to go if you want to remember the information for any longer than the exam itself (if you even last that long.)

With accelerated learning, you are going to break down what you are learning into practice sessions, and give yourself time to deliberately study what you are trying to learn with focus. They say that practice makes perfect, and here is where you get to put that to the test first hand.

Don't be a drag – part of the reason many people are unable to remember much of the middle of a given lecture is the fact that they have lost interest in the lecture by that time, and their minds are wandering to other things.

To combat this, accelerated learning puts something interesting in the center of the lecture, which means the student is going to remain focused on what is going on with the material, rather than allowing their mind to drift elsewhere.

Get creative – the final pillar that accelerated learning is built upon is creativity. This is the part of the learning process that will very much aid in you retaining the information you have learned, no matter how long you want to remember it for.

As you can see, accelerated learning is so much more than just studying something for the short term. This is a learning style that is designed to teach you how to learn anything – from academics to technical things to mechanics, or even in the artistic and musical realm.

This learning style is meant to break through all stigmas and barriers that we have all put up when it comes to learning, and erase the feeling of **I can't** and instead leave a person with the feeling of **I can and I will!**

CHPTER 15: OTHER TYPES OF INTERVIEW QUESTIONS

Remembering that each interview situation will be different will help you in the long run to find your own personal interview style. The best way to get better at interviews is simply to continue to interview. Take as many interviews as you can because at the end of the day the more you practice something the better you become.

You can also practice with someone in a role playing situation or talk to yourself in the mirror. Doing this will help you establish the base answers to common questions and will give you a sense of confidence that you know what you are doing. Confidence is a key element in producing a good interview.

The questions provided in this book are examples of some of the most common questions asked, however, there will always be variations of these questions. When you practice the interview process you will have the ability to ingrain in your mind many different forms of the questions and the responses which you can provide.

There is a chance you may have interview questions which are weird or out of the ordinary. Some questions are meant to stump the interviewer. This is not meant to be malicious but simply the interviewer wants to view how the interviewee will react under pressure and what kind of creative answer they may provide. Here are a few uncommon questions you may be asked.

If you could throw a parade of any caliber through the office, what kind of parade would it be?

How lucky are you and why?

If you were a pizza delivery man, how would you benefit from scissors?

If you could sing one song on a vocal contest show, what would it be and why?

Are you more of a hunter or a gatherer?

If you were a box of cereal, what would you be and why?

Do you believe in Bigfoot?

Why is a tennis ball fuzzy?

What is your least favorite thing about humanity?

How honest are you?

When you are eighty years old, what will you tell your children?

You are the newest addition to a crayon box. What color would you be and why?

If there was a movie produced about your life, who would play you and why?

What was the last gift you gave someone?

What is the funniest thing which happened to you recently?

Have you ever been on a boat?

What superpower would you like?

If the company was having a potluck, what would you bring?

Did you know that it costs seven million dollars to hire someone in this position?

How will you transform society for the betterment of all people?

Some of these questions are meant to throw the interviewee for a loop. Some of them are meant to give a more personalized view of the potential employee. When these types of questions are asked the interviewer is looking for creativity and honesty in the response. They are looking to get to know the interviewee on a deeper and more personal level while remaining professional.

It is as important to prepare for the weird and off color interview questions as it is for you to prepare for the common ones. Being unprepared for questions such as these will only leave you sitting quietly without a response which only makes you feel more awkward in an already stressful situation. There are many questions which can be asked of you and sometimes the interview is only questions such as these.

The reason an interviewer would ask only weird questions instead of the common questions covered in this book is because perhaps they have already made up their mind about you based on your history and credentials. Asking questions which will result in a reaction or a more creative response will provide your hopefully future employer with a more raw look into your emotional personality and capability to respond to questions which are jarring and off putting.

The key in these situations is to remain calm. Questions which are a matter of opinion have no right or wrong answer. While the interviewer may have a different opinion than you it does not mean your response is incorrect. Take a deep breath and look your interviewer in the eye. If you feel stumped do your best to avoid giving that away and bide yourself a little time.

Saying something like, "That is a very interesting question. Let me think about that for a moment." Will show you have not completely shut down upon them asking a question which was not expected. Most of these odd questions are created to assess your critical thinking skills. Explaining your reasoning for each of your responses is important to show your thought process behind your response.

Avoid answering questions which appear to be **yes** or **no** or are only one word, with only one word. Elaborate on your response with more details as to the how and why which will give your potential employer the knowledge that you are a detail oriented person. Employers are not looking for one word answers and should you fall into that trap you are demonstrating an incapability to think on your feet.

Employers want to see an active process of critical thinking when getting a response to their questions. Critical thinking is important in a job because it demonstrates the ability to think logically and quickly while obtaining results with the best possible outcome. Someone with good critical thinking skills can be trusted to make choices on their own and does not require a babysitter to perform their job duties. Critical thinking is highly sought after in every industry.

If critical thinking is listed as a keyword in the job description for the listed position it is a good indicator you may be asked more questions which are geared toward assessing this skill. Critical thinking requires an ability to be analytical. People with the ability to analyze have the skills to examine information, understand what that information means, and what it represents. Analytical skills require the person to ask thoughtful and meaningful questions about the situation, analysis of data, seek out more information when needed, interpret that information, use good judgment, question the evidence at hand, recognize differences and similarities, and use skepticism in a polite manner.

Also needed to be effective in critical thinking is an ability to communicate. It is an important skill to be able to communicate your needs and ideas to your team mates and your supervisors. This also demonstrates critical thinking within a group setting. In doing so you will need to be able to ask important questions, use your power of assessment of situations, collaborate with others, explain and express your point of view and ideas, have good interpersonal skills, be able to present to a group in a clear and effective manner, work as a team, use clear and concise written and verbal communication with care to use manners and decorum.

Another highly sought after aspect is creativity. You may need to spot patterns within information you are given or come up with solutions to issues no one has been able to prior. Being able to look at situations and problems from another point of view and find ways to solve the issues is a creative process. Creativity includes cognitive flexibility, conceptualization, curiosity, imagination, make and understand abstract connections, make inferences, predictions, synthesizing, and use of the power of vision from the point of view of the company, the project and the team.

Being open minded is another aspect of critical thinking which will open many opportunities within your career path. Being able to put aside your own assumptions and judgments and analyze only the information given helps when in a creative and a logical problem solving process. Being unbiased with a talent in being objective and evaluate all ideas presented is necessary in being open minded. You will also need to embrace different cultural perspectives, be fair towards others, remain humble, be inclusive of everyone in the team, remain objective, use observations and aid the function of the team through leadership skills, and the use of reflection to ensure everything has been thorough.

Finally problem solving skills will be necessary in your critical thinking. Being able to find solutions on your own without constantly needing a managers input is valuable. When problem solving you will need to provide a capability to apply the standards of clients and the company to situations and projects, have attention to detail, be able to clarify, collaborate with others, make decisions, evaluate progress and the situations you are working with, remain grounded and stay on task, identify patterns, be innovative, and use logical reasoning.

Companies which work with a broad base of different cultures will be on the lookout for your knowledge and openness of a new world view. They will also be looking for people who show an active interest in learning about those other cultures. It is a good idea to research the company in question and find out what cultures they currently have relationships with and with whom they are expanding.

Now that we have covered some bizarre interview questions, let us get you prepared for some other interview questions you may be asked which are in the same vain as the more common questions. It does not hurt to be over prepared and you can rely on a few standards when it comes to interview questions. Having responses already in your head can make the interview process go smoother and raise your chances of getting the position you are interviewing for. When you go into an interview you should have a clear layout in your mind of what you want the interviewer to know about you and the basic information you are going to say. Stuttering or saying, "um," or behaving in a dumbfounded manner, will not help you earn the position.

CHAPTER 16: Additional Exercises to Improve Your Speed Reading Skills

Implementing and trying out one or more speed reading techniques I've discussed in Chapter Four should be more than enough to get you started. But if you are still in need of more advice, this chapter is for you. Contained here are quick tips and exercises to help you keep the ball rolling.

Always focus on blocks of words and not individual ones. This is the very foundation of speed reading. Learn to read a whole sentence with just a quick glance instead of reading it word per word.

Keep a relaxed posture and position when reading something whether it's a book or an article on a computer screen or any digital device. Bad posture can cause all sorts of inconvenience on your neck and head. This in turn will significantly affect your concentration.

Always carry a book or an ebook reader with you so that you can practice speed reading anywhere. You can practice speed reading while commuting to work or while waiting for your kid at school.

Practice speed reading in an environment where there are as few interruptions and distractions as possible. The place should be quiet so that you can concentrate on reading. A library would be a great place to do your speed reading exercises.

Read both fiction and non-fiction books when you practice speed reading. In most cases, it's much easier to speed read a non-fiction book than a fiction book. This is because for fiction books, you often need to read every sentence to make sure that you are getting the flow of the story's plot and direction.

Go easy and don't rush your exercises. As I've said numerous times in this book, learning how to speed read takes time and patience.

Stop vocalizing the words when you read. This is the biggest reason why a lot of people take forever to read a book. As much as possible, you should prevent your lips from moving when you are reading.

Try covering the words and sentences that you've already read. When reading, there's a tendency for your eyes to keep reverting to paragraphs that you've already read. To help you solve this problem, you can use an index card to cover the sentences as you read downwards.

Train your eyes to make fewer movements. If you move your eyes too often while reading, you will be wasting precious seconds which can accumulate to minutes.

Never forget to look at titles and section headings. A heading offers an overview of what the succeeding paragraphs will be about. If you read them first, you will get an idea of what follows. Needless to say, you will be able to comprehend the text much easier.

Practice, practice, practice. You will only be able to improve your speed reading abilities if you practice. It's the only way to achieve the results you want.

All of these tips are not in any way difficult to follow. There's no reason why you shouldn't put them to practice, and start taking action today!

Chapter 17: Why Memorization is Difficult and How to Help Yourself

With research it has been determined that there are about 11 characteristics of information that determine how difficult or easy something is to memorize. Armed with the knowledge of these various characteristics you will hopefully be able to identify why certain knowledge it easier to retain while you struggle in other areas. After you have been given these characteristics will go over strategies that can help you improve memorization with information containing the various characteristics.

☐ Abstractness, this characteristic refers to how easy it is to wrap your head around the concept. If the concept is abstract in a nature it will be harder to relate to and make it all the more difficult to put into terms that you will be able to easily understand. The harder an object is to understand the more difficult it is to remember.

167

☐ Complexity, how complex or difficult a problem is can certainly determine how difficult it can be to retain. The more intricate the information the harder it will be for your mind to remember everything in its proper place.

☐ Familiarity, is how much exposure you have had to the information you are trying to retain. If you are memorizing information on something you interact with on a day to day basis it will be easier to remember information about it.

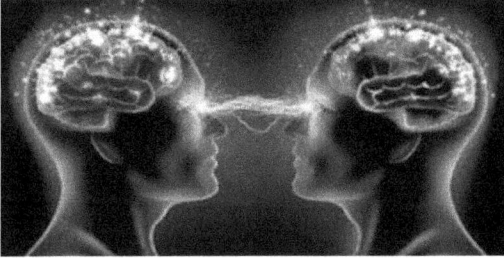

☐Humanness, this characteristic refers to how relatable a subject is to the human experiences in life. The more relevance a subject has to being human or experiences we face as human beings the easier it is to relate to and retain.

☐ Immediacy, how soon information needs to be retained. The shorter the time frame that information needs to be memorized by the harder or easier it can be to retain depending on your personality.

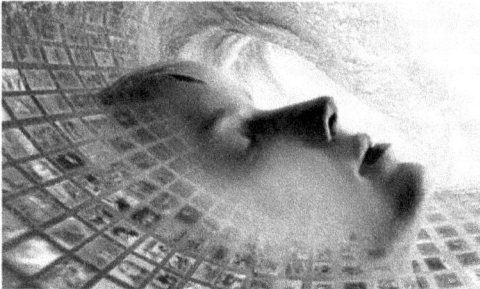

☐Importance, this characteristic points to how much the information you are trying to memorize impacts your life. The more important it can be to your life in any way can make it easier to remember.

☐Order, the more logical the structure of the information the easier it will be to retain. The more convoluted the information and the harder to decipher its proper order the more difficult it will be for you to remember. Our minds immediately seek to make things easier for us to understand, so if the order doesn't make sense it will be harder for our brains to retain.

☐Relevance, the more useful information will be to you the easier it will be to retain. If its something you can use in your everyday life or can help you in your endeavors the odds are it will be easier to memorize.

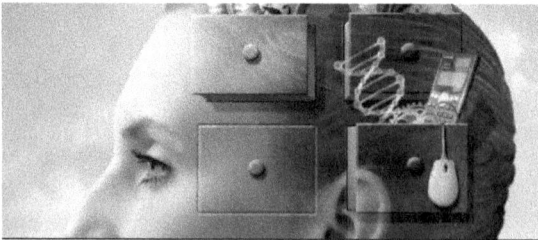

☐ Salience, when we find information boring it makes it that much harder to focus on the subject. When your bored in class you fall asleep, a similar thing can happen to your brain. When it's bored it can fall asleep in a sense and make it more

difficult to retain what your attempting to.

☐ Sensuous, how your senses receive the information you want to learn will help to determine how much easier it is to retain. If you can sense it on more planes it is more likely you will be able to remember it.

☐ Size, this characteristic can easily be seen as one that helps determine your retention of something. The more their is to retain the more difficult it can be.

Now that we have talked about how these characteristics affect how easy or hard it can be to retain information we will go over ways in which you can improve in areas you might struggle in. If you add characteristics to the material you are trying to retain and you discover a pattern to the types of material you struggle with then you can use these tips to hopefully help you overcome your shortcomings in that retention area.

☐ Abstractness, try to relate the information to what's around you. If you can find a way to make it less abstract and easier to relate to the everyday it will be that much easier to remember.

☐ Complexity, if you break it down into smaller pieces or simpler steps it can make it easier to understand and retain.

☐ Familiarity, try to review information more frequently. If you can try to review it for a short amount of time every day. The more you are exposed to it the more familiar you will be with it.

☐ Humanness, turn your information in a story and try to make yourself the main character. Not only will it help you relate the information to something more natural. By making yourself the star it will be all the more interesting to remember.

☐ Immediacy, setting yourself a deadline to have information retained by can help keep you motivated even if you don't need it for any particular time. Sometimes if you don't need it for a test or something similar you may procrastinate on the material in question.

☐ Importance, try to set a goal or objective to memorizing the information. If you can make it more important to yourself, it will be easier to retain.

☐ Order, if you struggle to remember information and the order makes no sense simply restructure it in a way that makes sense to you. You will then be able to better retain the information.

☐ Relevance, if you figure out a way in which it can be relevant to your life it will make it easier to retain.

☐ Salience, try to create a story to go along with the information. If you can string the information together in a funny or crazy way it will not only be more memorable but it will keep it more interesting.

☐Sensuous, if you can only associate your information with one sense you may find it harder to retain but if you try to find other sense that it can relate to you will find it easier to remember. It may take a little creativity to figure out how to engage other senses but it can be a big help.

☐ Size, if you have a large amount of material to cover break it down into smaller chunks to give your brain a more manageable chunk of information to remember.

When memorizing information most people use familiarity in order to retain information. Others who are better at retaining information.

Chapter 18: Accelerated Learning: The Future

Accelerated learning is a type of learning that involves learning in a much more efficient manner. It is a way of learning that was introduced within the 20th century and has helped society broaden horizons simply because it offers people something outside of the mainstream. Throughout history, every individual has always been offered learning at the same speed and thoroughness as everyone else. Accelerated learning offers diversity. If an individual or business excels in an aspect of life, accelerated learning offers them that bridge that can take them further than any mainstream type of learning ever could. Many believe it is hard to predict, but anyone could make the case that accelerated learning is the way of the future.

The Future

It is hard to tell what the future of accelerated learning will be like. One thing that is easy to tell is that accelerated learning or an improved form of it will be prominent in the future. Accelerated learning is so great because it gives an individual the opportunity to excel even more so than they already may. This is important because throughout history, no one actually had this opportunity. We do, however. This is why we as a race have excelled and learnt so much more in the past two hundred years than we ever did for the other thousands of years on this earth. We changed the way that we learned.

A Faster world

One thing that may be easy to predict is that accelerated learning will only become quicker as we delve deeper and deeper in future. If you look at human trends throughout the past two centuries, the one thing that we have done is gotten into a great big hurry when it comes to every aspect of life. People expect to have their food within minutes or it is taking too long. Cars and planes and boats have made travelling insanely quick. It was only a matter of time before the expectations to learn quicker and more efficiently became relevant as well.

Perhaps this is what is in store for us in the future. Accelerated learning will become the new mainstream type of learning, and accelerated learning will be replaced by a new concept that allows us to learn quicker than we can already learn at the moment. This may be troubling, because it shows that we are not truly cherishing the time that we have which in turn may desensitize us and make the human race more dangerous. One thing that is definite, is that only time will tell.

Chapter 19: Speed Reading- Picking Up the Pace for Faster Reading and Comprehension

Speed reading is a tool that, once learned, can be applied in almost any learning setting and plenty of real-life situations, too. The premise is simple- to train the brain to process the written word at a fast pace, allowing for quicker study and retention. Before we get to some exercises, let's go over the steps necessary to get started with speed reading.

It All Starts with Your Eyes

Assuming that you are reading this book in English, you are reading from left to right.

Slowly read this sentence, taking note of how your eyes move as you go. Is it one fluid motion, or do you find your vision jumping around a bit? The first step to training your brain to speed read is training your eyes to run smoothly and quickly over the written word. The goal is to practice scanning until your eyes learn to move as fast as possible. By doing this, you'll be strengthening and building endurance in the muscles that control eye movement.

Eliminate Subvocalization

Subvocalization is the involuntary internal pronunciation of the words on a page. We transition to doing this when we first graduate from reading aloud to reading to ourselves as children. For example, when we are reading a novel, we tend to say the names of the characters in our heads as we read them. That's often why when we see a movie based on a book, we might get upset to hear a character's name pronounced differently than we'd imagined it.

Sometimes, when we are subvocalizing, our lips will move silently as we read. In order to take up speed reading, you'll need to discover how to completely eliminate subvocalization. It's the first, but also the highest hurdle, in learning to read quickly. Once you've figured it out, the rest of the steps should follow with more ease.

To avoid and eventually eliminate subvocalizing, we need to venture into the abstract. Start isolating words as you read them and deliberately try to understand them without having to pronounce them to yourself. That may sound a bit weird, but it will work after time. As your brain becomes more accustomed to seeing words without saying words, you'll be able to pick up the pace. It's going to take a couple hundred words to start getting used to not needing to 'hear' them in your head.

Figure Out Your Starting Point

The only way you'll be able to track your progress as a speed reader is by determining your base. Speed reading is most often measured in pages per minute. A good way to figure out your baseline speed is by choosing a standard size novel, like a paperback, and turning to the interior, making note of the page number. Start a timer for five minutes, and start reading. When the timer goes off, see how many pages you've read. The average reader will have finished just one page. A speed reader would have completed two or three. There are, of course, online resources to help you determine your base, as well.

Over the course of an entire book, a speed reader will consume the text in a quarter to a third of the time of an average reader. Spanning over a longer period of time, the amount of reading material taken in by a speed reader can exponentially dwarf that of the average reader. If you'd like to track your speed reading progress electronically, there are websites and applications which test and record your speed reading results over time. If not, you can simply retest yourself after you feel your regular study sessions have started to take hold.

It IS Polite to Point

Using a pointer, a pencil, or your index finger to follow text as you read is perfectly acceptable in speed reading. It may seem counterintuitive or even childish, but one of the primary concepts behind speed reading is to be consistent. Using a tool to run along the line of text will help you take in each word at a steady speed. Consistency is key to mastering the art of speed reading, so try to move your tool at a constant speed with a smooth motion. This takes a little practice, but if you start slow, you'll soon find your eyes coordinating with your pointer as second nature.

Stay in Control

Control is another founding principle of speed reading. In order to become a proficient speed reader, you'll need to learn to control your impulse to skip ahead to the 'important stuff' and cause yourself to backtrack. Backtracking costs time and comprehension. While not all words hold the same weight (more on that next), not all books are created of the same content, and require differing levels of attention.

A pedantic textbook is not going to go down as smoothly as a beach-read novel. It's important to remember that the two components of speed reading are **speed** and **reading**. The reading itself is the more vital part of the process, so be aware that you may not get the same numbers on that textbook than you will on that cheap paperback, because the material in the textbook has greater weight and requires more critical comprehension. What is crucial, though, is that you can control your speed relative to the book you are reading to maintain consistency. Think of it like a dog show, where the dogs are being judged against their breed standard, not against each other.

Don't Sweat the Small Stuff

The little words don't matter. Seriously, they really don't. When we read at an average pace, our brains already skip over the small words- the articles and prepositions, the ifs ands and buts. Those words don't contribute much to a sentence, and we don't need to read them. Observe the sentences below:

- Tim went to the supermarket for milk, eggs, and bread.

- Tim went supermarket milk eggs bread.

The first sentence is written out in proper sentence structure; it has a full subject, predicate, and all the appropriate connectors and punctuation. The second sentence is what the speed reading brain should see. It's not pretty, but the meaning is not unclear. The speed reader still knows what Tim did.

Training yourself to eliminate these words is not nearly as difficult as eliminating subvocalization. Just practice slowly as you deliberately skip over these words until your brain just doesn't see them anymore.

Scanning and Skimming Your Way to Success

Now we're back to the big P- practice, practice, practice. The only way to improve your speed reading skills is by using them. Take up reading large chunks of information as quickly as you can, then figure out if you learned anything. The more you scan and the more you skim, the more you will train your brain to take in the important information as you go. Be sure to test your progress either manually or through a website or phone application.

What's the Bigger Picture?

Speed reading is a wonderful skill, but if you're not sure why you're using it, you need to stop and consider what the ability means to you, personally. Will you be able to learn non-fiction data at a quicker pace, allowing you to study faster and complete learning goals? Do you want to read your way through the fiction section at your local library? Do you need to buzz through a backlogged pile of periodicals or trade journals?

Speed reading can open all those doors for you, and so much more. Below, you'll find some exercises to get you on your way to success.

Speed Reading Beginner's Exercises:

Training your eyes- Forget about reading at all for now. This exercise is designed to develop strength and control of the eyes and eye muscles.

1- Look straight ahead and focus on a point in front of you. Turn your head slowly to the left, but keep your eyes on the fixed point. Now turn your head to the right. Repeat five times, slowly.

2- Stop focusing on the fixed point. Now turn your head to the left, without moving your eyes, allowing your vision to stay in line with the direction of your head. Turn your head to the right, in the same manner. Repeat five times slowly.

3- Bring your head back to center, looking straight ahead again. Leaving your head still, move your eyes slowly to the left, and then to the right. Repeat slowly five times.

You'll begin to notice how the motion of your eyes is relative to the motion of your head. Practice these eye movements regularly, but continue to pick up speed. You want to focus on the way your eyes move when you keep your head stationary (step 3). That's the muscle memory you will need to effectively scan left to right as you speed read. Work on developing speed and consistency of movement.

Training your brain-

Subvocalization is the most difficult thing to eliminate when learning to speed read. If the isolation technique in the chapter text doesn't work for you, try this: listening to music while you read. By splitting your attention between the sound of the music and the words on the page, you'll begin concentrating less on what the words 'sound' like.

Getting to the reading part-

To actually get on the road to speed reading, you'll need know your base speed, calculated from the method found above in this chapter. Next, you'll want to pick a couple of books or articles with similar content or a comparable reading level. Try choosing two novels by the same author or two long-form pieces from the same magazine. Pick one to start with.

1- Take ten minutes to read, at your normal reading pace. You are reading for content, clarity, and comprehension.

2- Read the same content again, this time trying to read the same amount in six minutes. Concentrate on the words, not the content. Use a pointer or your index finger as a guide.

3- Take a breather, then do it again, this time in 5 minutes.

4- Do it again- but in 4 minutes.

5- Congrats! You've just completed your first speed drill!

6- Take out your second piece of reading material. Read it for ten minutes at your normal speed. When the ten minutes is up, see how much you've read and calculate your page per minute speed.

You should already be showing an improvement from your original baseline. Practice this fifteen-minute exercise every day to see a steady increase in your pages per minute. Signing up for a speed reading testing website is a great way to track your progress electronically. There are many to be found with a simple search.

One of the things we discussed in this chapter was how to determine the necessary words in a sentence. In the next chapter, we'll take a deeper look at selective learning to speed up the study process.

Chapter 20: How to Improve Your Sleep Routine to Improve Your Brainpower and Memory

We all know that we think best and with clarity when we feel well rested. Getting quality sleep for one or two days does not help you achieve the target. You need to build a habit of sleeping well regularly to think clearly and with a peaceful state of mind every day. An alert and clear brain helps you learn, focus, and retain information better. Moreover, adequate sleep allows you to consolidate different pieces of information, perceive them from different angles, and from this, unlock the creativity you need to think of novel ideas and solutions to challenges.

As opposed to this, when you feel sleep deprived, you are unable to think clearly, focus attentively, and quickly grasp information. When you are sleepy and grumpy, you are also likely to commit more mistakes than usual. Healthy sleep on a regular basis puts you in the right and peaceful state of mind to be receptive to information and process it easily. Moreover, as you already know, sleep triggers various changes in your brain that help solidify memories.

To enhance your brainpower and the ability to memorize and retain information, here are some things you should do to improve your sleep habits.

Sleep for 6 to 8 hours daily at night

As shown by various research studies, adults need 7 to 9 hours of quality sleep on average daily to optimize their brainpower, self-discipline, and stamina. Some research studies also suggest that those who sleep for 9 or more hours regularly have poor memory as compared to those who get 6 to 8 hours of sleep daily on average.

If you are sleeping 2 to 5 hours on average daily, you are likely to feel exhausted, inattentive, and irritable. That is the reason why you struggle with memorizing things as well.

Track your sleep hours for about 3 weeks and find the average number of hours you sleep regularly. If you sleep for 8 to 9 hours once a week, but for barely 5 hours daily, that does not fulfill your body's sleep requirements. Focus on sleeping for at least 7 hours daily and if you do that regularly, it is alright if you sleep for 9 or more hours or even less than 5 hours every once in a while.

In this chapter, we will be discussing several potent tips to help you make the best use of sleep to improve your brain power as well as tips to enable you to fall asleep easily.

Nap before an important event

Studies have also shown that napping before an important event improves your analytical thinking and decision-making abilities, and your ability to remember information easily.

Every time you have an important event where you would like to perform well but especially remember information successfully, make sure to take an hour long nap a couple of hours prior to it. If you have to present a seminar at 8pm, nap around 12 noon for 20 minutes. After a nap, you are likely to feel fresher and more active.

Memorize information before going to bed

As mentioned earlier in the book, a study showed how participants recalled information better after getting some sleep once they completed memorizing it. If you wish to maximize your productivity and perform well on your tasks, learn things, review your To-do list, and work on your plans before going to bed daily. This way, you will recall all your plans easily the next day and will thus minimize your chances of forgetting important points.

Moreover, if you wish to come up with out-of-the-box solutions to some tricky problems or challenges, think creatively, or imbed important information in your mind, think of those things right before sleeping at night. Your brain is designed to hold on to information suggested to it right before bed time and processes it better while you sleep. This explains how often people come up with solutions to their issues on waking up the next day.

Reduce your caffeine consumption later in the day

Caffeine is great and we are definitely not telling you to kick it out of your life because hey, what is life without some guilty pleasure☐? That said, it is advisable to cut back on your caffeine consumption later in the day.

A single dose of caffeine, such as a cup of coffee, stimulates your brain, improves your focus, boosts your energy, and helps you stay alert. However, that happens when consumed in the morning or noon. When consumed later in the day, say past 5pm, coffee just stimulates your nervous system and keeps it from relaxing. In nature, mornings are ideal for work while evenings and nighttime are ideal for relaxation. If you stimulate close to when you need to unwind and rest, you will struggle with falling asleep.

197

It is all right to consume caffeine in the evening or night occasionally, but if you do that regularly, you will affect your sleep routine. A study showed that regular consumption of caffeine around 6 hours before bedtime drastically worsens your quality of sleep. Caffeine stays in the bloodstream for around 6 to 8 hours, which means if you consume huge amounts of coffee or tea after 4pm, you will only end up tossing and turning in bed at night. If you have strong coffee cravings in the late afternoon, evening or night, have decaffeinated coffee, but even then, do not make this habitual.

Reduce your exposure to blue light in the evening

There is a reason why the sun shines bright in the day and the moon beams softly at night: because your body is in such a manner that it needs strong daylight to stay active and less light in the evening to unwind and relax. If you expose yourself to strong light in the evening and night, you mess up your circadian rhythm, which tricks your brain into believing that the day is still going on. This affects the levels of melatonin in your body; melatonin is a hormone you need to sleep.

Make sure you cut back your exposure to artificial light in the evening and night; this includes the blue light emitted by screens such as TV, laptop, tablets, and mobile phones. Do not use screens at least 2 to 3 hours prior to your bedtime and keep the lights in the house dim and soft to relax, and get the good night's sleep you need to keep your brain healthy and active.

Set a proper sleep routine

Sleeping through the night is difficult at times when you do not have a fixed sleep routine. If you sleep at 11pm one night and wake up at 7am, but sleep at 12am the other night and wake up at 6am and keep changing your bed and rising times every other day, you will struggle with maintaining a healthy sleep routine and quality. You must have a fixed bedtime and rising time, and you need to stick to it for a couple of weeks until your body and mind adjust to it.

Keeping in mind your schedule and routine, set a bedtime and rising time that allows you to sleep for 7 to 8 hours and stick to it vehemently for a few weeks. Even if you kept tossing and turning in the bed at night for a few days, if you decided to wake up at 6am, do so. Similarly, even if you had a strong urge to stay awake until late and watch your favorite movie, do not pay heed to the urge; instead go to bed at 10pm as planned.

It takes self-control to sleep and wake up at set times even when you do not feel like it; understand that this is what your body needs. You need to stay in charge of your temptations and mind to make sure you function properly. Remind yourself of what a good night's sleep does to your brain every night before going to bed and sleep on time. Soon enough, you will build the habit of going to bed and rising early, and will notice a remarkable improvement in your brain health, cognition, focus, and productivity.

Exercise

Regular exercise and physical activity is by far one of the most important things you can engage in to stay fit, active, healthy, and strong. Working out regularly provides your brain with a healthy flow of blood that improves its functioning and health.

In addition, exercise and physical activities improve the production of feel good hormones such as dopamine and serotonin. These hormones improve your enthusiasm, happiness, and confidence allowing you to think well. This naturally improves your ability to focus and memorize things better.

Exercise for at least 40 minutes for 3 to 5 days a week. You do not have to start at exercising for 40 minutes per session right away. It is best to go about this goal gradually by starting with doing a rigorous physical activity for just 10 minutes.

You could brisk walk, jog, run, do aerobics, yoga, or Pilates, play a sport, dance or do anything else that helps you get active, sweat and feel energized. Build on to this habit by increasing the duration by 5 to 10 minutes every 2 weeks. In about 6 to 8 weeks, you will be exercising for a good 30 to 60 minutes 3 to 5 times a week, and you will be healthier and mentally stronger.

As stated earlier in the book, build a habit of these practices because good habits are how you yield positive outcomes. The next chapter discusses another important aspect you must work on to improve your cognition and memory: mindfulness, a tool that helps you become mindful, focused, and productive.

Conclusion

My hope is that you've found value in these simple methods for improving your learning speed, comprehension and memory. And more than simply being informed, I hope that you will apply what you've read, that you may be able to get excited about that brain of yours and use it to benefit others along the way. After all, knowledge is only potential power, and knowing is only half the battle.

You don't have to apply everything at once. Choose one or two lessons that you feel are most relevant or could prove to be most helpful to you, then apply it consistently for a couple of weeks until you've made it a habit. Then apply another one, and so on. Sometimes, the fastest way to learn is to go slow.

Here's to your accelerated learning success, my friend! Cheers!

www.ingramcontent.com/pod-product-compliance
Lightning Source LLC
Chambersburg PA
CBHW060319030426
42336CB00011B/1129